To Dad,

Merry Christn

Love

Christine

— x —

C000259211

THE
COLCHESTER
BOOK
OF
DAYS

SIMON WEBB

First published 2013

The History Press
The Mill, Brimscombe Port
Stroud, Gloucestershire, GL5 2QG
www.thehistorypress.co.uk

British Library Cataloguing in Publication Data.
A catalogue record for this book is available from the British Library.

ISBN 978 0 7524 8286 6

Typesetting and origination by The History Press
Printed in India

January 1st

2012: The Colchester Royal Grammar School became an academy on this day. This means that rather than being controlled and financed by the local authority, the school will be funded directly by the government in Westminster and also free to seek funding from private sponsors.

The origins of Colchester Royal Grammar School date back to the thirteenth and fourteenth centuries. The school has had a sound academic reputation for many years. Since the end of the Second World War, it has faced two serious threats to its existence. The first was in 1966, when Colchester Council tried to force the grammar school to become a comprehensive. Essex County Council rejected the plans and for the next decade, things went on as before. Then, in the late 1970s, the then Education Secretary, Shirley Williams, drew up plans for the abolition of all the remaining selective schools in Britain. Pupils from Colchester Royal Grammar School marched through the town in protest. As it turned out, the Labour government fell in 1979 and the plans for doing away with grammar schools were abandoned by the incoming Conservative administration. The school has come first in the A level league tables every year since 2006. In 2004, the BBC named it as being the top state school in the entire country.

January 2nd

1892: On this day George Biddel Airy, who held the post of Astronomer Royal for an incredible forty-six years, died. He was born in Northumberland in 1801, but his family later moved south and young George attended the Royal Colchester Grammar School. He was an enormously popular pupil there, chiefly because he had a technical bent which enabled him to make extraordinarily effective peashooters!

One of Airy's greatest achievements was the establishment of the Prime Meridian at Greenwich in 1851. A few years after his retirement, he had the satisfaction of seeing this adopted as the international basis for timekeeping and navigation; a position which the Greenwich Meridian still holds to this day.

It was not only in astronomy that George Airy excelled. Years before he became Astronomer Royal, he devised a method of calculating the Earth's density. His first attempt to do this – at the age of 25 – failed, but he later managed to experiment with two pendulums, one deep within a mineshaft and one on the surface. By discovering that gravity at the bottom of the shaft exceeded that on the surface by 1/19286, he was able to show that the specific density of the Earth was 6.566.

JANUARY 3RD

1837: This is the day that William Westwood, aged 16, appeared at the Essex Quarter Sessions in Colchester, accused of stealing a coat. He was convicted and sentenced to an unbelievable fourteen years' transportation to Australia. Once there, he became a bushranger, more or less a highwayman; one of the most famous in Australia. His nickname was Jackey Jackey and one of his peculiarities was that he never harmed his victims. Some called him 'The Gentleman Bushranger', partly because of his courteous manner when dealing with his victims and partly because of his habit of carrying out his robberies dressed in a smart suit.

Jackey Jackey became a legend. He was captured several times, but always managed to escape. In 1845, at the age of 25, he was caught and brought to court, where he was sentenced to life imprisonment in the notorious penal settlement on Norfolk Island. The following year, he led an attempted breakout, in the course of which three police officers were killed. On October 13th 1846, William Westwood was hanged.

JANUARY 4TH

2005: The *Evening Gazette* reported on this day the finding of the only chariot circus ever unearthed in this country. The discovery, in Colchester's Abbey Fields district, led to demands that the town should apply for World Heritage status.

Most people are familiar enough with Hollywood epics such as *Ben Hur* to know what a Roman circus would have looked like; an elongated oval track where chariots would race round, while the crowd placed bets on the outcome. The excavation revealed some of the most important parts of Colchester's circus, for instance the starting gates and obelisks which marked the turning points at either end of the track. Calculations showed that the stadium contained seating for an astonishing 8,000 spectators – probably the entire population of Colchester during the third century AD. In other words, there was room for every adult in the whole city to attend the races!

The future of these unique remains was to be buried beneath a huge new development, although, at the time of writing, the Colchester Archaeological Trust have moved into a building on the site and hope to open it to the public soon.

JANUARY 5TH

1958: On this Sunday evening, a Dutch au pair called Mary Kriek disappeared. She got off a bus only 100 yards from the farmhouse at Eight Ash Green, Colchester where she was living and working, but never arrived home. The next day, her body was found ten miles away. She had been beaten to death and her killer was never caught.

The murder of Mary Kriek provides an early case of press intrusion. Complaints were made to the Press Council that reporters from British newspapers besieged the home of Mary's parents in Holland, pestering them for their reaction to the violent death of their daughter. Letters appeared in *The Times* about this case, most people being deeply critical of the behaviour of the press. *The Daily Mirror*, which had refused to print photographs of the grieving parents, published an editorial in which they denounced the intrusion into private grief which was becoming so common in the 1950s. One cameraman from a British newspaper had even tried to arrange for a photograph of Mary Kriek's parents as they left the mortuary after viewing their daughter's body.

JANUARY 6TH

1850: This was the day that Charles Haddon Spurgeon, probably the most famous preacher Britain has ever known, converted to Christianity. Sixteen-year-old Charles, who was born in the Essex town of Kelvedon, was on the way to an appointment when a snowstorm caused him to take shelter in the Methodist chapel in Colchester's Artillery Street. In his own words, 'God opened my heart to the salvation message'. He was received into the Church three months later and baptized on May 3rd 1850.

By the time he was in his mid twenties, Spurgeon had become the most popular preacher in England. At times, he preached to 10,000 people at a time, hiring music halls for the purpose of teaching people about the Bible's message. So popular was he, that an enormous Baptist church was built in south London, of which he became the pastor. The Metropolitan Tabernacle is still standing and has room for 5,000 worshippers at a time. His sermons were printed and circulated like newspapers. When Dr Livingstone died in Africa, it was discovered that one of his few possessions was a copy of one of Spurgeon's sermons.

Charles Spurgeon continued to preach regularly, despite his increasing ill health. He died in 1892, at the age of 57.

JANUARY 7TH

1831: The local newspaper, the *Essex County Standard*, was launched upon this day. The first local newspaper to cover events in Colchester was *The Essex Mercury or Colchester Weekly Journal*, which began in 1733. It was published by John Pilborough, a bookseller with a shop in Colchester High Street. It was popularly known as 'Pilborough's Journal' in order to distinguish it from the *Ipswich Journal*, which also carried news of Essex at that time. *The Essex Mercury* folded in 1747. After that time, the *Ipswich Journal*, which ran until 1771, had a column of news from Colchester and the surrounding districts.

Colchester's next local paper was the *Colchester Gazette and General Advertiser for Suffolk, Norfolk, Cambridgeshire and Herts*, which began publication in 1814. It was initially published by Swinborne & Co. in the High Street, but changed hands three times in nine years, absorbing the *Colchester Courier* in the process. Various other newspapers based in Colchester were started at this time.

When the *Essex County Standard* began in 1831, it was described by the publishers as, 'a standard around which the loyal, the religious and the well-affected of our County may rally'. It is the only local paper which has lasted and is still being published today.

JANUARY 8TH

1735: Thomas Twining was born on this day. His father, Daniel, was a famous tea merchant in London – Twining's Tea is famous to this day – but Thomas found no pleasure in the world of commerce. He preferred academic study to buying and selling tea, and so ended up at Cambridge University. He took Holy Orders at the age of 29 and a few years later married Elizabeth Smythies, daughter of one of his teachers at Colchester Grammar School.

After his marriage, Twining became vicar at Fordham, a small village near Colchester. He remained the vicar there for the rest of his life, although in later years he was also the vicar of White Notley and, from 1788, the Rector of St Mary's in Colchester. He moved to Colchester from Fordham in 1790.

In addition to being a priest, Thomas Twining was a noted musician and classical scholar. He assisted Charles Burney in the writing of his *History of Music*. Burney's daughter, Fanny, said that Twining was, 'besides being deep in musical knowledge, a man of great humour and drollery'.

JANUARY 9TH

2007: Peter Pearson saw a hummingbird hawk moth feeding – or, to use the correct technical term, nectaring – on Viburnam flowers in the garden of his house in Chalfont Road, Colchester on this day.

So important was the hummingbird hawk moth's appearance in Chalfont Road at this time of the year that the news was headed 'Stop Press' on the website of the Colchester Natural History Society. We learn that this is without doubt the earliest sighting of this moth in not just Colchester, but the whole of Essex! It was seemingly an over-wintering specimen, at least according to the improbably named Joe Firmin, who has been keeping an eye on such things since 1952.

January 10th

1986: The first ever episode of the popular television series *Lovejoy* was broadcast on this day. Jonathon Gash, the author of the *Lovejoy* stories, lives in West Bergholt, just outside Colchester. Jonathon Gash, whose real name is John Grant, set the stories of the lovable rogue of an antiques dealer in Essex and much of the filming for the television series was in North Essex. Some scenes were filmed in Colchester itself, for example at the town's railway station.

The *Lovejoy* television series turned parts of Essex into tourist attractions. Coaches came to villages and towns like Coggeshall and Finchingfield, just to see the places where filming had been done. Jonathon Gash is still writing Lovejoy books; the most recent, *Faces in the Pool*, being published in 2010. The possibility of remaking the television series surfaces regularly. It would hardly be possible to use the original star of the programme; Ian McShane is now 70. David Hassellhoff, the American actor who starred in the 1980s series *Knightrider*, has expressed interest in taking on the role, although the author of the original books is said to be a little dubious about the idea.

January 11th

1965: This is the day that the Queen approved the grant of a charter to the University of Essex. Essex was for a time in the sixties the archetypal 'Plate glass university'. At one time, universities in industrial cities such as Manchester were termed, in a slightly disparaging way, 'Red brick universities'. In 1968 Michael Beloff coined the expression 'Plate glass universities' to describe some of the newer institutions which had sprung up in the 1960s. Chief among those which he singled out for mention were the University of Kent, University of East Anglia and of course the University of Essex. Beloff called them by this term because they seemed to him to consist of little more than expanses of concrete and plate glass.

Actually, there is something of an irony about this particular designation for the University of Essex. Far from being built only of concrete and glass, the residential blocks for students on the Colchester campus were the tallest load-bearing brick structures in the world when they were opened in the 1960s! None of the so-called red-brick universities have been able to match this brick-related feat.

JANUARY 12TH

1969: On this day, the first meeting of the Colchester Hammond Organ Society took place above a shop selling pianos and Hammond Organs in St Botolph's Street in Colchester. George Fulcher, 'a classically trained church organist with an interest in the electronic organ', had been appointed manager of the shop on November 5th 1968 and was raring to start a Hammond Organ society as soon as he could identify and locate enough fellow enthusiasts.

The inaugural meeting attracted twenty prospective members for the projected club and has never looked back.

Apparently, interest grew so rapidly that the room above the shop in St Botolph's Street was soon too small to accommodate all those Hammond Organ players and it was found necessary to move round the corner to Priory Street, where a handy church hall was to be found. According to the society, 'many famous organists played for us there', which included Keith Beckingham, Len Rawle and Ena Baga. The Colchester Organ Society is still going strong, over forty years later, although they dropped the 'Hammond' from their title some time ago.

January 13th

1338: From this date, Colchester Borough was obliged to hold courts three times a year. Before this, the administration of justice in the town was apt to be somewhat haphazard and irregular. From 1338 though, courts began to be held at Michaelmas (September 29th), the Feast of St Hilary (January 13th) and on the second Tuesday after Easter.

In addition to these regular court days, bailiffs were appointed who could hold 'inquests' at other times. Today, we tend to think of an inquest as being only concerned with an unexpected or suspicious death, but the early inquests of the sort held in Colchester were interested in minor matters of law; they were really the forerunners of our magistrates' courts. William le Salter and Ida Hotfot, for example, were caught buying eight mullets before the fish market had officially opened; an offence against the trading laws of the time. The bailiff had them arrested and held an inquest on the matter that very morning. The penalty was that they should lose both the mullets and the money which they paid for them; which amounted to 1s 9d. They were also warned that if they were caught breaking the law in this way in the future, then they would both be liable to be set in the pillory.

JANUARY 14TH

2012: On this day, a lively discussion began on the *28DL* website about the proposed demolition of the old Odeon cinema in Crouch Street, Colchester. The Odeon, which opened in 1931, closed down as a cinema in 2002. A planning application was made in 2008 to convert it into a nightclub, but this was rejected by Colchester Council. The Odeon is not a listed building, although it is regarded by Colchester Council as being notable. Steve Peri, who owns the Art Deco building, said that he had given up on the idea of converting the all but derelict Odeon into a nightclub and was now thinking in terms of knocking it down and developing the site as shops.

Members of the *28DL* site – the title references the film *28 Days Later*, a post-apocalyptic British zombie film – are what are known as urban explorers. They have any interest in entering, absorbing the atmosphere of and photographing derelict old buildings; the creepier the better. At least one of those commenting on the proposed demolition of the Odeon had evidently been into the place since it had closed down. He reported that the interior was still very impressive, although now coated with pigeon droppings. The suspicion was expressed that the disused cinema had been allowed to deteriorate in order to encourage the council to permit its demolition.

JANUARY 15TH

1681: Lady Thamar Shaw, daughter of Samuel Lewis of Royden in Suffolk, died on this day. Lady Shaw's connection with Colchester is an interesting one. During the seventeenth and eighteenth centuries, it was the custom that when an important person died, his or her coat of arms was painted in oils and hung over the doorway of the house for a year, during the official period of mourning. After that, it would be given to the church where the person had worshipped, in order to be hung there. These paintings were known as hatchments and were usually in a lozenge-shaped frame.

Holy Trinity Church in Colchester contains five hatchments, one of which is that of Lady Thamar Shaw. The arms were constructed in a rigid and formal way, which enable many deductions to be made about the circumstances of the deceased. For instance, in Lady Shaw's hatchment the background of the Shaw side of the arms was white, indicating that her husband was still alive when she died. We know this to be true in any case, because, opposite Lady Shaw's hatchment, is that of her husband, Sir John Shaw, Recorder of Colchester and MP from 1659-1661. His date of death is recorded as being in 1690; almost a decade after that of his wife.

JANUARY 16TH

2011: On this day, Malcolm Mitchell made a Freedom of Information request to Essex County Council about the number of automatic cycle counters in Colchester. One of the great pleasures of Freedom of Information requests is that they let us know just how little we *do* know about the affairs of our town. The average person was probably not even aware that there were such things as automatic cycle counters, let alone that there might be enough of the things to warrant a Freedom of Information request to identify them.

There is something faintly Orwellian about the idea of machines counting every bicycle which passes down a street. Why would anybody want to know this information? There are nevertheless dozens of the things all over Colchester; each one busily engaged in automatically counting each passing bike and tallying up the scores so that they can be forwarded to the council. While they were counting cycles, they were also keeping track of mobility scooters, pushchairs and any other wheeled contraption which was not powered by an engine.

JANUARY 17TH

1722: John Smorthwaite married for the second time on this day. Although born in Westmoreland, John Smorthwaite did his best work in Colchester, where he arrived in 1712. He was a fully trained and proficient clockmaker and spent the next twenty-five years or so making clocks in Colchester.

It is not widely known that Colchester once had quite a tradition of clock making; a tradition for which Smorthwaite provided much of the impetus. One of his apprentices, Nathaniel Hedge, went on to become a well-known clockmaker in his own right. This was after he had made Smorthwaite's daughter Sarah pregnant; an action which led to both Hedge and Sarah being thrown out of John Smorthwaite's house and left out of his will.

Today, Smorthwaite's clocks and also those made by Nathaniel Hedge are eagerly sought after by collectors. Smorthwaite was quite a wealthy man when he died in 1739. In addition to a fine house in Magadalen Street, which he left to John Smorthwaite, a relative of his in London, he also bequeathed some oyster beds to his niece. It is said that over 300 fine clocks are still in existence which were produced in Colchester during the eighteenth century.

JANUARY 18TH

2010: A witness to strange phenomena in the sky over Lexden, Colchester, posted an account of his experiences on the UK UFO Sightings website on this day. The man, who gave his name only as Ben, had seen six orange lights moving across the sky. These had also been observed by a couple of his colleagues. A little later, five or six aeroplanes appeared from different points in the sky and seemingly all headed south-west, in the direction taken by the mysterious orange lights. According to Ben, the lights had been travelling approximately three times as fast as the planes, which he supposed had set off in pursuit. The point was made that the lights were completely silent.

There is probably nothing really inexplicable about this sighting. It was made at night, which makes judging relative heights and distances difficult, even for those who are experienced in such matters. In other words, it would have been impossible to gauge accurately whether the lights were 3 feet wide and at an altitude of 200 feet, or if they were 300 feet wide and at an altitude of three or four miles. The former guess is most likely the case: almost certainly these were Chinese lanterns; miniature hot air balloons, which, when released, float across the sky until the candle burns out. They are generally orange and move with the wind.

JANUARY 19TH

1963: On this day, John Bercow, the Speaker of the House of Commons since June 2009, was born. After attending a large comprehensive school in Finchley, Bercow decided that his ambitions lay in politics. Before this, he was the top junior tennis player in Britain. A severe bout of glandular fever put an end to his sporting career. After leaving school, Bercow decided to study Government at the University of Essex near Colchester. This university has a reputation for political activism dating back decades, and in the 1960s was at the forefront of the so-called Student Power movement. Demonstrations against the war in Vietnam, sit-ins to protest about Britain's work on chemical weapons; some people were heard to express surprise that the students at this university found any time at all for studying amidst all their political activity. This fiercely left-wing reputation made it a strange choice for the teenage Bercow, as he was even then an avowed Conservative. Nevertheless, he stayed at Essex for three years, graduating with a First Class Honours degree in Government in 1985. Professor Anthony King described him as an outstanding student, although 'very right wing and pretty stroppy'.

January 20th

1680: Jacob Ringer, bays maker, died on this day. He was buried in St Martin's churchyard in Colchester.

At one time, Colchester was one of the most important towns in Britain for the manufacture of cloth from wool. This work was principally carried out by Flemish weavers who settled in the town in the fifteenth century. They lived mainly in that part of modern Colchester known as the Dutch Quarter.

Readers are probably puzzled as to where 'bays' comes into this? In fact this is the old spelling for the material we know today as baize; the soft felt which is used to cover snooker tables. The Colchester weavers did not work in factories, but in their own homes. Some of the older houses in the Dutch Quarter have very large windows at the front to allow a lot of light in. In the days before electric lighting, a plentiful supply of natural light was essential for those carrying out fiddly work at their looms. In the late eighteenth century, things changed with the mechanisation of weaving and it died out as a cottage industry.

JANUARY 21ST

2012: On this day, a ghost hunt was held at the Red Lion pub in Colchester. People paid £40 a head for the chance to track down spectres and the spirits of the dead. They could hardly have chosen a better location than the Red Lion for this purpose, for it has a long history of haunting. Built in 1465, it is supposedly home to several ghosts.

In 1638, Alice Katherine Millar was murdered at the Red Lion. Her ghost became such a nuisance that in the early eighteenth century, the then owner of the inn had the doorway to her old room bricked up to stop her passing in and out. It was a fruitless effort; she now simply passes through the solid brickwork! Another well-known phantom is that of a small boy who apparently haunts the Parliament Room of the Red Lion. He is especially likely to be seen by children and has allegedly appeared in a number of photographs taken in the pub.

For the last century or so, there has been a standing rule at the Red Lion that any staff claiming to have seen ghosts, or who even talk about the subject, will be liable to instant dismissal. In recent years though, this strict regime seems to have been relaxed and the management are now only too happy to welcome those who wish to search for the long dead residents of this old inn.

JANUARY 22ND

2009: A review of the book *Rude Britain* appeared in *The New York Times* on this day. What has this to do with Colchester? Only that one of the nearby villages which make up the borough of Colchester features in the book. The community of Fingringhoe lies about five miles from the centre of Colchester. Although nobody can quite place their finger upon it, the name does sound vaguely obscene, which is why it is listed in *Rude Britain* as being one of the twenty rudest place names in the country.

Writing her review of the book for *The New York Times*, Sarah Lyall expresses her amazement at the endless willingness of the British to giggle at their more unusually named towns, villages and streets. Mind you, in some ways the inhabitants of Fingringhoe have got off lightly. Another village in Essex must take first prize as far as embarrassing names are concerned. The village of Ugley, not far from Epping, has caused many red faces. The Women's Institute uniquely gave the branch of their association in this village permission to call itself 'The Women's Institute of Ugley'. The general rule is that the name of the place precedes the words 'Women's Institute'. It was felt that few women in the village would have wished to be members of the 'Ugley Women's Institute'!

JANUARY 23RD

2012: The *Harwich and Manningtree Standard* reported on this day that paratroopers from Colchester were receiving training to deal with rioters, in case they were called upon to help police in the future. During the rioting which swept the country in August 2011, there were calls to deploy the army on the streets of England's cities, but the government chose not to do so.

Members of the 3rd Battalion, the Parachute Regiment spent two days in a special training centre in Kent during January. While there, they were pelted with bottles, rocks and petrol bombs; practicing tactics to restore order. Despite speculation in the national press that this training could be put into effect if there was a repetition of the 2011 riots, officers from the Parachute Regiment remained vague about the purpose of their visit to Kent. The officer commanding A Company said, 'As the Airborne Task Force, we are on standby to go on operations anywhere in the world at short notice. As well as conventional war fighting, we could be involved in disaster relief or civil disturbances, and that might require dealing with hostile crowds.'

JANUARY 24TH

1577: On this date a terrible murder was committed at New Hythe in Colchester. It has become a case which is often used to demonstrate the rule of law in Elizabethan England.

Alice Neate lived with her husband, daughter Abigail and her husband's sister, whom she hated. On the night of January 24th 1577, Alice crept into her sister-in-law's bedroom and cut her throat. She then wrapped the body in a red blanket and dragged it out of the house and hid it in the woodyard. Her trial was a model of judicial fairness. The alibis of various visitors to the house that day were carefully examined, as was testimony from Alice Neate's husband and daughter. It was her daughter's evidence which clinched the case. At first she steadfastly declared her mother's innocence, but eventually broke down under cross-examination. Young Abigail shared a bedroom with her aunt and had been awake during the murder. The case against Alice Neate could hardly have been clearer and it is little wonder that she was convicted of murder and later hanged. Her trial shows that all the main features of modern justice were already established by the time of the Tudors.

JANUARY 25TH

1915: On this day, British forces landed on the Gallipoli Peninsula in Turkey. Among the soldiers was the vicar of the Essex island of Mersea. The padre of the 5th Essex Infantry Brigade was the Reverend Charles Pierrepont Edwards, who had been appointed the vicar of Mersea in 1898.

Reverend Pierrepont had for a time been a curate in an East End district not noted for its respectful attitude to the clergy. He started a boxing hall and was happy to get in the ring with the roughest young men. This earned him the nickname of 'The Fighting Parson'. Although as a vicar he was not liable to be called up during the First World War, he volunteered almost as soon as war was declared. So unusual was this, that the King himself asked to be presented to 'The Fighting Parson'.

After winning the Military Cross at Gallipoli for rescuing injured men under fire, Revd Pierrepont returned to his duties in Mersea. He continued in the post of vicar there for an amazing forty-eight years. It was not until he had witnessed a second World War that he finally ended his career as Mersea's vicar. Even then he did not retire, his long service being ended only by his death in 1946.

JANUARY 26TH

1560: The earliest record of the surname Cordy is to be found in Colchester on this day. Cordy is an unusual name and is probably related to the Norman French *Lecordier*; a maker of cords or string. For some reason, possibly connected with the weavers who lived in Colchester from the medieval period onwards, this name seems to be more common in Essex and Suffolk than it is in the rest of the country. Variant forms are Corday, Cord, Cordee and Cordie. The very first written record of the Cordy form of this name is when Mary Cordy, daughter of Jonas Cordy, was baptised in St Botolph's Church on this date.

The earliest mention of any variation of the Cordy or Corder name in Britain also occurs in East Anglia. In 1182, a William Cord is found in the records of Abbot Sampson at Bury St Edmunds in Suffolk. Perhaps the most famous Corder from this part of the country was William Corder, the murderer in the notorious Red Barn case of 1828. Corder, whose nickname at school was 'Foxey', was born and bred in Suffolk. He murdered his mistress rather than marry her and was eventually hanged at Bury St Edmunds on August 11th 1828.

JANUARY 27TH

2012: Those with £25 to spare could have paid to attend on this day a three-hour course in Colchester on how to use a pendulum. This workshop, which promised to 'tap into your intuitive abilities and release the energies that are with you', seemed pretty comprehensive and to cover all aspects of the use of the pendulum. Topics included cleansing and blessing your pendulum, preparing and protecting yourself, and balancing Chakra. By the end of the three hours you would have been taught, 'all that you need to know to make your pendulum a tool that you won't want to live without'. A dazzling prospect indeed!

The same outfit who teach the use of the pendulum, Links Eternal, will also put you in touch with a spirit guide and instruct you in the use of tarot cards.

JANUARY 28TH

2012: Visitors to Colchester Zoo received a practical lesson in nature study on this day. Colchester, like many zoos these days, organises regular displays of birds of prey flying free above the spectators. One of the most popular turns at such shows are owls. These predators are completely silent in flight and a well-known party trick is to have them swoop a few feet above the audience's head. Of course, the term 'predator' is relative. Owls might be fierce enough when attacking field mice, but weighing only 19oz limits their ferocity somewhat.

The birds of prey display at Colchester on this day went smoothly enough until somebody took a flash photograph of a performing barn owl. This spooked him and he ended up flying into a window. Dazed, he then flew off to recover, making a terrible error in thinking that the best place to do this was the nearby lion enclosure. When a 550lb lion meets a 19oz bird, the outcome cannot be in doubt for long. A lioness batted the hapless owl in mid air, knocking it to the ground where another lion pounced and gobbled it up in a single mouthful. The zoo apologised for the mishap.

JANUARY 29TH

1858: On this day, a report appeared in the *Essex County Standard* about the sale of an obelisk standing in Colchester High Street. The obelisk, which had stood as a milestone since 1760, was being moved because the road was to be widened. It was sold to Mr Charles Wire of Magdalen Street for £3 5s 0d or £3.25 in today's money. What did Mr Wire want this tall and ornate stone marker for? The curious answer is to be found in Colchester Cemetery.

What use Charles Wire found for this large block of granite for the first thirty years or so after purchasing it, we do not know. When his wife died in 1889 though, the old milestone reappeared, suitably engraved with Mary Ann Wire's epitaph and planted prominently in the cemetery, where it stands to this day. Whatever possessed Mr Wire to buy the thing in 1858? Did he simply see a bargain to be had, buying it on spec as it were and only later deciding to use it as his late wife's gravestone? Or did he perhaps plan all along to put it to this use? It is certainly no ordinary milestone, being very tall and beautifully carved. The mystery is unlikely ever to be solved at this late stage.

JANUARY 30TH

2004: The film *Warrior Queen*, which shows the destruction of Roman Colchester, was released in Finland on this day. *Warrior Queen*, starring Alex Kingston as the eponymous heroine, is regarded by some as the worst historical film of all time. Commenting on the IMDB site the day after this film was first shown on British television, one viewer said, 'Appalling. A total work of fiction, no semblance of historical accuracy at all'. Others were not so kind. 'The dialogue was twisted, the facts unrealistic', 'easily one of the worst historical films I've ever seen', 'never known so many inaccuracies in one programme'; the comments just get worse and worse.

The only notable part of this film is that it features Colchester, albeit thousands of years ago. For some reason, Colchester is not popular with television and film producers. With the exception of an episode or two of *Dr Who* set in the town, the only film where one may catch glimpses of Colchester is *The Fourth Protocol* (1987). This thriller, based on a Frederick Forsythe novel and starring Michael Caine, has a number of street scenes filmed in Colchester.

JANUARY 31ST

1953: On this day, the North Sea began to flood the Essex coast. A combination of a high tide, exceptionally low atmospheric pressure and high winds caused the death of over a hundred people living on the coast. Thirteen thousand people were made homeless by the floods; making it one of the worst natural disasters ever to hit this country.

Although the worst effects of the flooding were at Canvey Island and Clacton, Mersea Island was also badly affected. The causeway, known as the the Strood, was under 6 feet of water. The gale-force winds piled up the water and propelled it along the estuaries of the Colne and Blackwater. This resulted in some flooding at Hythe, near Colchester, and even as far inland as Manningtree. No lives were lost in Colchester or the surrounding area; damage was limited to property. In Wivenhoe, for instance, a number of cellars were flooded.

In 1993, a flood barrier was erected on the River Colne to protect low lying land in the event of another event like that of 1953. There was strong opposition to the barrier from those who felt that it might interfere with their hobby of sailing, but the Colne Barrier was built anyway.

FEBRUARY 1ST

1836: Lexden and Winstree Poor Law Union was formed on this day. The year that the Poor Law Union was formed, they arranged for the building of a new workhouse. Some of the old almshouses which had previously accommodated the poor were really quite cosy and no worse to live in than any other small cottages. Parishes also gave what was known as 'outdoor relief'; in other words money and food for poor people so that they could continue to live in their own homes. The new Poor Laws ended all that. The idea was essentially to make life so difficult and unpleasant for those who applied for help that they would prefer to go without. The new workhouse that Lexden and Winstree Poor Law Union built was designed with just this in mind.

The Lexden workhouse was built to the same design as a number of prisons which were being erected at that time; the so-called 'panopticon' plan. In this type of prison, the corridors radiate from a central hub, enabling staff there to keep an eye on everywhere at once. Pentonville Prison in London is a good example of a panopticon prison. That the same plan should be adopted for a workhouse says a lot about how the poor of Lexden were viewed at that time! The workhouse later became St Albright's Hospital and is still standing.

FEBRUARY 2ND

1777: On this day the *Ipswich Journal* advertised cock fighting at the Waggon and Horses public house in Colchester. The advertisement claims that:

> At the Waggon and Horses in Colchester on Wednesday, March 5th, will be fought a main of cocks, the Gentlemen of Suffolk against Gentlemen of Essex, shewing 21 mains for Five Guineas a battle and Ten the odd Battle.

Cock fighting has been around for at least 3,000 years in India, from where it gradually spread to Europe and America. It was tremendously popular in eighteenth-century England, with fortunes being gambled on the outcomes of fights. The five or ten guineas quoted above is absolutely nothing; whole estates changed hands at this time on cock fights. Roosters are naturally aggressive to each other and the ones used in this sport, known as gamecocks, were specially bred for stamina and strength.

The Waggon and Horses seems to have been a favourite venue for this type of entertainment, because later, in 1777, the *Ipswich Journal* was carrying more advertisements trying to attract custom for cock fighting. On December 10th that year, for instance, sixteen cocks were being fought, including one which was three years old. No cock was to weigh more than 4lb 10oz and all entrants were to pay the landlord ten shillings for each rooster entered in the fights. It was apparently something of a money spinner for the landlord!

FEBRUARY 3RD

1636: The Swan Inn was sold on this date by Martin Basil. It was bought by John Beriffe, described as 'a gentleman'. It is evident that he decided to convert the place into a private home.

The Swan stood in Frere Street, which was later renamed East Hill, and the earliest record of it is when reference is made in some court documents to 'the Swan Hospice' in 1539. In 1541, Robert Stampe of Colchester and his wife Joan registered the sale to a baker called John Damsell, 'all that tenement or hospice called "le swan", with cottage adjoining it, in St James' Parish Colchester, in the street called ferris-street opposite le Greyfrerys'. It seems clear from this that the name Frere Street was a corruption of Friars or Greyfriars.

The Swan stood just inside Colchester's East Gate and so would have been the first inn encountered by travellers from Ipswich and Harwich. This would have made it a busy and profitable establishment. In an old engraving showing Charles I's mother-in-law arriving in Colchester, the Swan can be seen, with a large carved model of a swan to indicate that it is an inn. It was demolished in the middle of the eighteenth century and no trace of it now remains.

FEBRUARY 4TH

1536: On this day Parliament received the *Valor Ecclesiasticus*, which resulted in the dissolution of the monasteries. Ostensibly, there was a religious motive behind this move, but the truth is that Henry VIII had not forgiven the Catholic Church for opposing his divorce. In addition to this, the monasteries were wealthy and Henry had designs upon their property.

St Botolph's Priory in Colchester was the first Augustinian priory church in England, being founded at the end of the eleventh century, only a few years after the Norman Invasion. St Botolph's was never a particularly rich or prestigious religious house, being very much in the shadow both physically and metaphorically of the larger St John's Abbey, which lay only a couple of hundred yards south of St Botolph's. Nevertheless, it was one of the first monasteries to be dissolved, ceasing to exist in 1536.

The remains of St Botolph's are impressive, even in their ruinous condition. There is no stone for building in Essex and so the fabric of the building is of lumps of flint, mixed with old Roman tiles. It is still a fine example of early Norman ecclesiastical architecture, although today only the main walls of the nave remain standing.

FEBRUARY 5TH

2011: A soldier from the 3rd Battalion Parachute Regiment, based in Colchester, was killed in Afghanistan on this day. As a garrison town, Colchester has for centuries been used to hearing about the deaths of soldiers stationed in the town. Every so often though, one of these casualties seems particularly poignant. Such was the case with Company Sergeant Major Colin Beckett, who was described by the officer commanding 3rd Battalion, Lieutenant Colonel James Coates, as one of the most talented Sergeant Majors of his generation.

Colin Beckett joined the army in 1990 and rose rapidly through the ranks, becoming in the process an expert in anti-tank warfare. He had, at his death, already served two tours of duty in Afghanistan, as well as having served in Kosovo and Northern Ireland. Sergeant Major Beckett's unit had come under fire on February 5th and three of the men, including Beckett, had been forced to take cover in a ditch. They had no way of knowing that an IED (an improvised explosive device) was concealed nearby. It exploded with devastating force, killing Beckett instantly. He left behind him a wife, Rachel, who was pregnant at the time of his death.

FEBRUARY 6TH

1967: Baron Alport of Colchester spoke in Parliament about southern Africa on this day, the year that he was appointed High Steward of Colchester. This is a ceremonial position which holds no real power or authority and is awarded as a mark of long public service to somebody who has some connection with Colchester. It was not always so. The second person to hold the post, the Duke of Albermarle, owned a plantation in Jamaica, where he also lived. Despite being appointed High Steward, he never set foot in Colchester!

Baron Alport had strong links with Colchester; chiefly the fact that he was, from 1950 to 1961, the MP for the town. Born Cuthbert James McCall Alport on March 22nd 1912, Alport was a career politician. From 1937 up to the outbreak of war in 1939, he was an assistant secretary at the Conservative Party Education Department. He fought in the war, being an officer first in the Royal Welsh Fusiliers and then the King's African Rifles. By the time the war ended in 1945, he was a General Staff Officer in East Africa. He became the director of the Conservative Political Centre in 1945, serving in that capacity until he was elected MP for Colchester in 1950.

After he left the Commons, Alport was raised to the peerage, becoming Baron Alport of Colchester. He was not only High Steward of Colchester for a time, but also Deputy Lieutenant of Essex. He died in 1998.

February 7th

2011: An aardvark was born at Colchester Zoo on this day. The zoo has one of the most successful breeding groups of aardvarks in Europe and the only breeding colony in the United Kingdom. This was the fifth baby to be born to this particular pair of aardvarks, named Oq and Adela. As soon as they were aware of the birth, zoo staff separated the mother and baby from the main enclosure and provided them with special quarters. Newly born aardvarks are very short-sighted and clumsy and if this step had not have been taken, there was a risk that the new arrival could have inadvertently been trampled underfoot. Even so, both mother and baby required twenty-four hour attention to ensure that the latest addition to the family was kept safe.

The separation of the vulnerable new aardvark was necessary for the first month, until the baby was able to survive the rough and tumble of life in the burrow. It would be some time before staff were able to come up with a suitable name for the baby aardvark, as telling the sexes apart is not really possible without a close examination. It was eventually discovered to be male and named Tatsu, which means 'dragon' in Japanese. Some indication of just how successful the breeding programme at Colchester Zoo has turned out to be is provided by the fact that this was the sixth delivery in the aardvark burrow to date.

FEBRUARY 8TH

1973: The *Colchester Echo* carried an article about the history of The Bull public house on this day. There has been a public house or inn on this site in Colchester's Crouch Street since at least the fifteenth century. The first records are of the building's owner paying tithes of three groats to the Abbot. There is a gap of several centuries and the next thing we know about The Bull is that the Market Sergeant was in the habit of setting up his office in the tap-room in order to collect the duty from foreign traders, who brought silk goods to the town to sell.

In 1791, William Coke, the son of the landlord of The Bull, was convicted of murder. He was sentenced to transportation for life to Botany Bay in Australia. While there, he became a respectable citizen, so much so that forty years later, in 1832, he was given a full pardon and allowed to return to his own country.

The Bull's heyday was the century or so before the railways came to Colchester. The Red Lion in Colchester was the inn for stagecoaches, but The Bull catered for the slower stage wagons. Travelling to Colchester in this way took three days or so and most travellers were thus ready for a drink and a bite to eat when they arrived!

FEBRUARY 9TH

2011: Sheila Parsonson MBE, who founded the Colchester and District Cat Rescue and Re-homing Society, died on this day. The Colchester Cat Rescue, known as CCR, began in 1974 at Great Tey, just outside Colchester. It was registered as a charity in 1978. In 1996, CCR moved to purpose-built premises on the road between Colchester and Ardleigh.

Apart from twelve individual 'chalets' for cats which are to be re-homed, there are three large groups of cats living at the CCR's headquarters. Some of these are feral and are likely to continue living there for the rest of their lives. No cat is ever destroyed, except on the advice of a vet. Any cat which ends up here is assured of a comfortable berth for life.

Sheila Parsonson lived in London until her late forties, working for an insurance company. In 1973, she took early retirement and moved to Great Tay. She had taken in stray cats while living in London – now she made it, quite literally, her life's work. In 2002, at the age of 76, she went to Buckingham Palace, where she was presented with an MBE by the Queen for services to animal welfare. In addition to the rescue centre, the CCR runs a charity shop in Eld Lane in central Colchester.

FEBRUARY 10TH

1754: Mary Webster died on this day. It was she who bought Colchester Castle as a present for her daughter, Sarah. Those living today in Colchester are so used to regarding the castle as more or less a public possession, that it seems a little strange to think of it being bought and sold in precisely the same way that we might a semi-detached house!

Colchester is the largest castle keep ever built in Britain; in fact it is the largest surviving example of a Norman keep in the whole of Europe. It is one and a half times as large as the Tower of London, the most well-known example of keeps of this sort. After surviving the Siege of Colchester in 1648, a survey two years later condemned the place and it was sold to John Wheely, a local ironmonger, who set about demolishing it and selling the remains for building materials. He managed to dismantle most of the upper storey with gunpowder, before the whole enterprise proved to be unviable financially. In 1727, Mary Webster bought the castle and gave it to her daughter. It then passed into the administration of Sarah's husband, Charles Grey, who was the MP for Colchester. At first, he rented half of it out as a barn and the other half to the authorities so that they could continue to use it as a prison. Later, though, he began an extensive programme of restoration.

FEBRUARY 11TH

2007: Two men arrived at a police station in the Suffolk town of Ipswich on this day and told the police that they had the body of a dead woman in the boot of their car. The corpse was that of Colchester woman Nicola West. Nicola had lived a blameless and unremarkable life growing up in Colchester. She attended Copford Primary School, before transferring to Stanway School at the age of 11. After leaving school, she worked at Pizza Hut in Colchester High Street. At the time of her death, she was working for St Elizabeth's Hospice. The story of how she came to be laying dead in the boot of somebody's car was a curious one, which took some time to untangle.

At first, Robert McCarry and Paul Waters, both unemployed, suggested that she had met her death during a sexual game which had gone wrong, in which she had consented to be partially strangled for erotic pleasure. This theory soon unravelled and police charged the two men with rape and murder. They were both convicted and sentenced at Ipswich Crown Court to life imprisonment. The judge recommended that McCarry should serve at least nineteen years in jail and Waters thirteen.

FEBRUARY 12TH

1971: Pink Floyd played at the University of Essex on this day. These days, we would expect a well-known rock band only to play at proper venues, but forty years ago it was not at all uncommon to find a big band such as Pink Floyd, playing at a college or university.

Pink Floyd's concert at Essex is notable for some of the more obscure songs which they played there. In addition to *Atom Heart Mother,* the album of which had only been released a few months earlier, and *A Saucerful of Secrets*, they performed songs such as *Careful with that Axe, Eugene.* This song, written originally for the soundtrack of the film *Zabriskie Point,* vanished from their repertoire a year or two later and is all but unknown to any but the most devoted fan of the group.

A bootleg recording of the concert at the University of Essex is still available and the list of tracks makes interesting reading, mixing as it does the familiar with the almost wholly unheard of. Who today remembers, for instance, *Astronomy Domine* or *Cymbeline*? The album produced from this concert makes for interesting listening, particularly when compared with their later work, relying as it does heavily upon electronic effects.

FEBRUARY 13TH

2007: This is the day that the world record for serving a portion of chips was set in Wivenhoe. Henley's fish and chip shop was acknowledged by the *Guinness World Records* as preparing the fastest chips in the world. It took staff at the shop a mere 3 minutes and 41 seconds, starting from a couple of potatoes, to peel, slice, fry, wrap and serve a portion of chips.

The *Guinness World Records* contains a surprising number of chip-related records, a number of which are held by this country. Another Essex town, Southend-on-Sea, now holds the record for the biggest ever serving of chips. Staff at the chip shop in the town's Adventure Island theme park took four hours and twenty minutes to prepare, fry and box an astounding 448 kilos of chips. That's almost half a ton! It is unlikely though that anybody will in the near future be able to beat another British record in this field; that of the largest portion of fish and chips. This too was set in this country, at West Witton in Yorkshire. An enormous single piece of halibut weighing 44lbs was served up alongside 57lbs of chips.

FEBRUARY 14TH

1896: At one time otters were very common in Essex and on this day one was discovered near East Mersea, which became the subject of a bizarre anecdote.

In the later nineteenth century, a book entitled *The Mammals, Reptiles and Fishes of Essex* was published. A lot of the information contained in it has been drawn from magazines such as *The Essex Naturalist*. It seems quite astonishing to us today that the great majority of the curious anecdotes related, end in the death of the animals being described. Otter hunts and the digging out of badgers so that they can be torn to death by terriers is talked of as though that would be the most natural thing in the world to do. The anecdote from East Mersea makes therefore a refreshing change.

It appears that otters were commonly seen along the Colne, from Brightlingsea and Mersea, all the way up to Colchester. One Mr Cole found a baby otter in a rabbit's hole near his home in East Mersea. He felt so sorry for it that he wrapped it up and took it home, where, incredible as it might sound, his cat suckled it. It was later released back into the wild.

FEBRUARY 15TH

1928: This day saw the drawing up by a solicitor of a notice announcing the impending liquidation of the Mersea Shell Crushing Company. The notice was duly advertised in the *London Gazette* and the company was wound up.

There seems to be something almost surreal about the idea of a company whose sole business entailed crushing shells. It becomes even stranger when one learns that the Ministry of Agriculture and Fisheries was closely involved with this company. As a matter of fact, the Mersea Shell Crushing Company was connected with both fisheries *and* agriculture.

To produce healthy eggs with hard shells, chickens need to absorb a lot of calcium in their diet. This is generally provided for them in the form of roughage like grit. Limestone contains a good deal of calcium carbonate and if the chickens are left to their own devices, they will sometimes peck about in the ground and pick up enough dietary calcium in this way. It is often necessary to provide them with a supplement and this is where the shell crushing comes in. Crushed shells of molluscs such as limpets are an ideal way for chickens to get calcium and the ground shells can simply be mixed with their feed. The shore of Mersea Island provided an endless supply of shells and so was ideal for such an enterprise.

February 16th

1911: This was the day that the first Royal Warrant was granted to Wilkin & Sons, the Tiptree company. Wilkin's have been producing preserves for over 125 years and today the company's products are as popular as they have ever been. The Wilkin family had already been farming in Tiptree for 200 years before they decided to go into the business of making jam and other conserves. In 1885, Arthur Charles Wilkin joined together with two business partners to form the Britannia Fruit Preserving Company. They scored an early success, when an Australian merchant was so impressed with their jams that he contracted to buy their entire output.

By 1901, the company had over 8,000 customers on their books. Four years later, the name was changed, because so many other companies had Britannia in their names. It became Wilkin & Sons Ltd; the name by which it is known today. In 1911, George V gave the company's products his official endorsement and ever since then they have been entitled to put the Royal coat of arms on their jars. By this time, Wilkin & Sons were exporting jam to every part of the British Empire and beyond.

Production at Tiptree reached a peak in the early 1920s, when over 200,000 customers were placing orders with Wilkin & Sons. Today, things are a little slower as changing fashions mean that jam and other preserves are not quite as popular as they once were.

February 17th

1662: Ralph Josselin of Colchester recorded on this day that:

> In the night it rained, the wind rose and was violent beyond measure overturning a windmill at Colchester wherein a youth was killed; diverse barns, stables, outhouses, trees, rending diverse dwellings. Few escaped. My loss much, but not like some others, God sanctify us all. Throwing down stacks of chimneys, chimneys, parts of houses. Lady Saltonstall killed in her bed, her house falling.

This terrible storm, which apparently caused a great deal of damage in Colchester according to other accounts, seems to have swept across southern England in just the same way as the hurricane of 1987. That it was not some localised freak weather can be seen from examining Samuel Pepys' diary for the same day. His experiences in London closely match those of Ralph Josseline:

> Walking in the streets, which were everywhere full of brick-battes and tyles flung down by the extraordinary wind last night, that it was dangerous to go out of doors; and hearing how several persons had been killed today by the fall of things in the street.

All of which indicates a storm verging upon hurricane-force which affected at least as much of the country as that of 1987.

FEBRUARY 18TH

1934: The Norfolk contingent of the Great 1934 Hunger March arrived in Colchester on this day and spent the night there.

The hunger marches of the 1930s are usually associated in the minds of those who are aware of them with the North of England or South Wales. Places such as Jarrow and Newcastle are well known for their contribution to these desperate protests against unemployment. The aim of the hunger marches, the first of which took place in 1932, was to draw attention to the plight of those who could not find work. There was no nationwide benefits system such as we know today and the families of unemployed men were quite literally starving. Since events in those parts of the country outside London and the Home Counties did not seem to matter quite so much to the government, groups of workers determined to travel on foot to London so that all the country could see their protests.

In the 1934 Hunger March, a large number of unemployed men assembled at Great Yarmouth on February 13th and slogged on foot to London, passing through Ipswich and staying overnight in Colchester. They then marched on to London, joining protestors from the rest of the country for a rally in Hyde Park on Sunday, February 25th.

February 19th

1888: A supposed case of Spontaneous Human Combustion took place on this day. On the evening of February 19th 1888, a soldier went into a hayloft at Mill Street in Colchester and settled down to a quiet smoke, combined with a heavy drinking session. When we learn that he also carried with him an oil lamp, the fact that a fire was later reported in the hayloft might not seem particularly surprising! What was odd though was that only the upper half of his body had been reduced to ashes by the flames. His legs were untouched and there was no sign of fire elsewhere in the loft.

The Colchester case is often cited as a perfect example of Spontaneous Human Combustion, in that the heat seemed to be confined entirely to the victim's body, without affecting the surroundings. Fire-fighters though know that the behaviour of fire can be quite unpredictable. It is not at all improbable that somebody could spill spirits on his clothes and that the fumes from this could ignite. It is worth noting that in this case, the soldier was drinking brandy. Simple accident seems far more likely than inexplicable phenomena.

FEBRUARY 20TH

1954: The inaugural meeting of Colchester and District Archery Club was held on this day. There had been a flourishing archery club in the town during the 1850s, but the last mention of it was in 1860. The *Field* magazine records that on July 2nd that year, a large party of archers gathered at Lexden to practice, following which they held a ball.

The present club was formed after Bill Tucker, who only arrived in the town the previous summer, arranged a meeting at the Town Hall for anybody interested in joining a local archery club. Tucker was a member of the Essex County Archery Association and there were apparently already twenty archery clubs in the county at that time. Archery enjoyed something of a craze in Essex during the post-war years and clubs were to be found at Southend, Woodford, Chingford and Walthamstow.

The Colchester and District Archery Club soon made a name for itself, putting on demonstrations at various fêtes and shows in Essex. In 1955, it was given permission to incorporate the borough arms in its badge. Today, the club meet every Tuesday in the summer at Mill Road sports ground. In the winter, they meet at Highwoods Sports Centre.

FEBRUARY 21ST

1915: The first air raid ever to take place in Essex happened in Colchester on this day. It was also the first time ever that an aircraft dropped a bomb on British soil. We tend to associate air-raids with the Second World War and it is easy to forget that Britain was pounded by the German air force quite extensively over twenty years earlier, during the First World War.

The first bombing of this country was carried out not by aeroplanes but by the huge airships called Zeppelins. From the end of 1914 onwards, Zeppelins visited this country and dropped bombs. Because all the raids of this sort were by airships, the first bombing from an aeroplane came as something of a shock. On the evening of Sunday, February 21st 1915, a Quartermaster-Sergeant of the 20th Hussars was sitting at home at his house in Butts Road, Colchester. His wife was just bringing dinner to the table, when there was a huge explosion at the back of the building. When they went to investigate, they found that all the windows on that side of the house had been blown out and that there was superficial damage to other houses in the street. On going outside, they could just see an aeroplane vanishing in the distance. Bombs were also dropped on Coggeshall and Braintree by the same plane.

FEBRUARY 22ND

1740: According to a report in the *Ipswich Gazette* on this day, Alderman George Grey of Colchester was to be removed from his post after being convicted of having gay sex.

George Grey was a plumber and glazier and the object of his affection was a barber. Both men came from Colchester. They had been caught actually in the act of having sex together and, after being arrested, had been remanded to stand trial at the Chelmsford Assizes. They had spent some time in the pillory and then returned home. A meeting of the council was held at the Moot Hall soon afterwards in which, to quote the *Ipswich Gazette*, 'It is desired by the burgesses that George Grey, plumber and glazier and Alderman of this town shall be removed from his office by reason of him being convicted of sodomical practices at the last Assizes'. No mention was made of his partner in crime, the barber, and it is a fair guess that he did not hold any sort of position in the town's life of which he could be stripped.

FEBRUARY 23RD

1839: William Peck was born on this day in Huntingdonshire. Every town has many worthy citizens whose fate it is to be remembered only for minor achievements in their own territory. William Peck was one such man. He was a woolen draper and hosier with a shop in Colchester High Street. Peck was a local councillor in Colchester whose chief claim to fame in his own lifetime was that he was instrumental in making bowls a popular game in the town. He presented a set of bowls to the Colchester Recreation Ground in the late nineteenth century and, although there was no official green at that time, the game soon took off; becoming tremendously popular on Saturday mornings.

The hosier died a few years later, acquiring a posthumous claim to fame of sorts. When Charlie Chaplain became the darling of cinema-goers, somebody remembered that Councillor Peck had been married to Lydia Gayford. She was actually a first cousin of Charlie Chaplain's grandfather, Spencer.

FEBRUARY 24TH

1950: On this date the Balkerne Gate in Colchester's Roman city wall was granted Grade I listed status. The Roman walls around Colchester are the best preserved in Britain, surviving to almost their full extent. Their most remarkable feature is the Balkerne Gate.

Before the walls were built around Colchester, a triumphal arch was erected to commemorate Claudius' entry in AD 43. This was incorporated into the walls when they were being constructed, along with a gateway for pedestrians. It is this which survives as the Balkerne Gate. Horses and wheeled traffic would have entered through the old Triumphal Arch, to which the Balkerne Gate was attached on one side. Where this stood is now a public house; the Hole in the Wall.

The Balkerne Gate has only been exposed to view in the last hundred years or so, which probably accounts for its almost perfect state of repair. It was probably blocked up at some stage during the Roman occupation and its name refers to this blocking; it was 'baulked' or closed up.

FEBRUARY 25TH

1789: On this day, there was a fight between smugglers and excise men near Mersea Island. The Essex coast near Colchester was a favourite place for smugglers to bring goods ashore, there being many suitable spots in the estuaries of the rivers Blackwater and Colne to land barrels of brandy and so on. On the evening of this day, a group of customs officers were on the watch for smugglers and noticed a line of horses and donkeys passing them, loaded with barrels and kegs. This was clearly worth investigating. In fact there turned out to be twenty gallons of brandy and another twenty gallons of gin in the barrels; all of which had recently been landed from France.

A brisk fight ensued when the smugglers were challenged, involving sticks and swords; one of the men in the melee, James Payne, being cut about the head badly. He escaped and with his friends sought medical attention. In the words of the doctor who treated them:

> I dressed the prisoner on the night of the 25th of February, about two miles from Manwood, at a house between Mersey Island and Manwood; I believe there were six of them all wounded; the general tenor of their conversation was that they had had an affray with the Excise officers in Manwood, and that they were all wounded; the prisoner was one of them.

At the Old Bailey later that year, Payne was sent to prison for two years; a light enough sentence under the circumstances.

FEBRUARY 26TH

1785: On this day, the *Ipswich Journal* carried a strange advertisement about the forthcoming election in Colchester. It said:

> The committee for collecting evidence in support of the petition against the Colchester election give this public notice, that they will continue to sit at the house of Shining Jemmy known by the sign of Neptune's Nag, every evening next week, in order to receive information. As facts will be difficult to obtain, any probable circumstances, or a plausible pretext will be admitted.

This puzzling notice was put in the paper by the landlord of The Seahorse, which, until 1935, stood at 61 High Street, Colchester. This was known facetiously in the town as 'Neptune's Nag'. The landlord, who was quite active politically, was really inviting anybody who felt like coming to the pub to gossip about politics, simply to turn up at the pub. In fact, the landlord divided his allegiance pretty equally between Charles Grey, the Tory candidate and his Whig opponent, Isaac Rebow.

The Seahorse was acquired in 1886 by the Colchester Brewing Company. For some reason, the licence for this house was refused in 1935, after which it was forced to close down. The Colchester Brewing Company sold the building to Mr Gadson of Adams Motors Ltd, who ran a business next door. The price was £2,600 and it was demolished the following year.

February 27th

1931: The Regal cinema opened in Crouch Street, Colchester on this day. It later changed its name to the Odeon. The Regal was designed by architect Cecil Masey, who specialised in cinemas and theatres. He designed over forty in this country before the Second World War.

While it was being built, a large sign advertised the fact that this was to be a 'super sound cinema'; talking pictures only having been introduced a year or two previously. The auditorium seated 1,446 patrons. As was the custom at that time, the Regal was elaborately tricked out inside, giving the auditorium the appearance of an Italian courtyard. A documentary was made of the building of the Regal, its construction having some points of interest for architects and designers. When it was completed, the site was visited by the Essex, Cambridgeshire and Hertfordshire Chapter of the Society of Architects.

In addition to films, the Regal had live shows, presenting itself as something like a cross between a cinema and a music hall. It was equipped with backstage dressing rooms, very much like a theatre. Its conversion in 1974 into a three-screen cinema put an end to the use of the stage.

FEBRUARY 28TH

1856: This was the day that recruitment ended for what was known as the German Legion. During the Crimean War, which began in 1854, the government realised that there were not enough British troops and so decided to recruit foreign mercenaries from other European countries. Some were Belgian and Swiss, but the majority were German. They were housed in prefabricated wooden huts in Colchester, which then became the first permanent garrison in the town. When the war ended, the British offered all the members of the German Legion who were married, posts in a new militia being formed at the Cape, in what is today South Africa.

Predictably, there was a mad rush among the members of the German Legion to acquire wives. Many single girls in Colchester, particularly those working in shops, found themselves being ardently courted by men who could hardly speak a word of English. In the space of two weeks, over 150 weddings were conducted between men from the German Legion and local young women. On the last Sunday before the German Legion was due to be disbanded, no fewer than sixty-four marriages were solemnised in the Garrison Church.

March 1st

1866: St Botolph's railway station opened on this day. Colchester's first station was built by the Great Eastern company in 1844. Because of the angle at which the line from Liverpool Street Station in London approached the town, siting the station in the centre of the town would have entailed constructing two bridges across the River Colne. Since these were the days when the first railways were spreading across the country at top speed, it was decided to place Colchester's station in the most convenient place for the builders of the railway, rather than the most convenient location for those living in the town who would be using the railway! The result was Colchester North Station; some way from the main shopping and residential districts.

Twenty years later, the Tendring Hundred Railway constructed a line from Clacton to Colchester. This was far more central, but took passengers only towards the coast, instead of in the direction of the capital.

In 1991, the name of St Botolph's Station was officially changed to that by which everybody in Colchester had known it for a century or so; that is to say Colchester Town. It is unusual in that trains have to drive in and then reverse out of the station. It has only one platform and is used by approximately 400,000 passengers every year.

MARCH 2ND

1936: This day marked both the end of Colchester Town FC and the start of the new team of Colchester United. Colchester Town Football Club had begun in October 1873; playing for the first twelve years in knitted jerseys rather than shirts. They were soon nicknamed 'The Oysters', a reference to the product for which Colchester has been famous since Roman times.

Colchester Town FC were amateurs and their players all had full-time jobs during the week. They were not the only football team in Colchester at that time; there was also the Excelsior Club. In 1890, the two teams agreed to amalgamate when playing serious matches and only to retain their individual identities for local games.

In the early years of the twentieth century, a new Colchester team emerged; the Colchester Crown. Colchester Town led a somewhat nomadic existence at this time, chronically short of money and often without a pitch either. At one point, they were using a pitch in Sheepen Road which had formerly been the municipal rubbish dump. In 1936, the committee running Colchester Town FC tried to set up a new professional team. At first they hoped to continue with Colchester Town playing as well, but the rules forbade this. The result was the end of Colchester Town FC in 1936 and the emergence of Colchester United the following year.

MARCH 3RD

2008: On this day, a mother and daughter called the police after seeing what they thought was a black panther on wasteland near Colchester General Hospital. According to their statement to the police, the creature was definitely not a dog and far too large to be a domestic cat. Some were swift to record this as yet another sighting of the so-called 'Beast of Essex'.

The Beast of Essex was first heard of in the Braintree area of Essex during the mid-1990s. It was apparently a large cat, usually described as being very dark and looking like a panther. Since those early reports, this mysterious creature has supposedly been seen in many other parts of the county, including a number of locations around Colchester. In 2007, for instance, there was a report of a large wild cat on Mersea Island and in January 2009, it was seen by a police officer in Wivenhoe.

Some of these reports are treated seriously by the police; on one occasion, a helicopter with thermal imaging was scrambled. Despite almost twenty years of sightings though, solid evidence has yet to emerge and the verdict currently must be one of 'not proven'.

MARCH 4TH

2005: Some members of the Woman's Union in the parish of All Saints with St Cedd at Shrub End in Colchester attended a Women's World Day of Prayer. The theme this year was 'Let our Light Shine' and it had been organised by women in Poland. The focus was upon bread and salt as metaphors for spiritual sustenance; as used in the Gospels. The concept of the Women's World Day of Prayer began in 1962, with ecumenical World Day of Prayer events.

A good time was had by the Women's Union, and they sang three hymns during the course of an informative talk.

MARCH 5TH

2011: On this day, a 'flash mob' event was organised at the B&Q store in Colchester. All B&Q stores in the country had decided to take part simultaneously in a fundraising event for the Comic Relief charity. The idea was that at the same time all across the nation, staff at B&Q would all spontaneously break into a dance routine to the music of Black Eyed Peas 'I've got a feeling'. An eight-minute long clip on YouTube shows how carefully choreographed the business was, with staff being dragooned into a practice session to make sure that they all knew the right moves to the music.

In the event it was a great success, with shoppers at the Colchester store staring in bemusement at the sight of the staff stopping work to sing and dance for a few minutes. Some curmudgeonly types were heard to remark that it took long enough in the ordinary way of things to get served in B&Q, without the additional delay of staff indulging in disco dancing. Judging though by the thousands of hits that even the video of the practice at Colchester received on YouTube, the general feeling was that it was a worthwhile enterprise.

MARCH 6TH

2011: Those citizens of Colchester with £35 burning a hole in their pockets could on this day have begun attending a series of five evening sessions which would help them to meet and get to know their Spirit Guides. You too could have turned up at Compton Road, Colchester and learned what signs to look out for so that you would know when your Spirit Guides were near at hand and trying to contact you.

Each of us have, apparently, more than one Spirit Guide and through meditations and exercise, you can learn to recognise each one of them individually and discover what area of your life they have been helping you with.

MARCH 7TH

1574: John Wilbye, England's most famous madrigalist, was baptised on this day. Wilbye was born at Brome in Suffolk. His father was a tanner and yet surprisingly, considering the poor family in which he grew up, young John showed a precocious ability for music from an early age. By the age of 20, he had acquired what any young man of modest means in the Tudor age needed to get on in the world; that is to say a wealthy patron. Wilbye somehow caught the attention of the Cornwallis family and he was invited to stay with them on many occasions. He even accompanied Elizabeth Cornwallis to her wedding when she married Sir Thomas Kytson in 1594.

In the sixteenth century, it was not at all uncommon for the aristocracy to have musicians, artists or philosophers actually living full-time in their mansions and this seems to have been the case with Wilbye. He published two sets of madrigals during Elizabeth Cornwallis' lifetime; one in 1598 and a second in 1608. When his patron died in 1628, a rather bizarre thing occurred. He was, in effect, inherited by her daughter. And so it was that he went in 1628 to live with Mary Darcy, Countess Rivers in Colchester. When he died ten years later, he was buried in the graveyard of Holy Trinity Church, near the city centre.

MARCH 8TH

1957: The *Essex County Standard* reported on this day that Colour Sergeant Major Frank Towery presented the landlord of the Prince of Wales public house with a shield to show his regiment's gratitude. What had Mr and Mrs Mead, the proprietors of the Prince of Wales, done to earn the army's recognition in this way?

When the 1st Battalion West Yorkshire Regiment took up their posting in Colchester, the NCOs made an alarming discovery. There was no Sergeants' Mess for them to eat in. As a result, the Prince of Wales became in effect the Warrant Officers and Sergeants' Mess for the regiment for the first year or so that they were stationed in Colchester. In addition to the ornamental shield, Mrs Mead was presented with a string of pearls by the grateful soldiery.

From the eighteenth century right up to 1990, the Prince of Wales was a popular public house in Military Road, Colchester; only a stone's throw from the barracks. It closed in 1990 and swiftly became ruinous. In 1993, it reopened as a jazz bar. This was quite an upmarket joint. It deteriorated though, until by 1999 it had become a lap dancing club. A few years later, it was converted into a Thai restaurant, which it continues to be at the time of writing.

MARCH 9TH

1893: A paper was read on this day at a meeting in Colchester about some Roman remains unearthed in Castle Park. They came to light during the landscaping work undertaken around the castle before the park was opened to the public. Apart from half a dozen skeletons which were found, thought to have been Saxon although the reasons for this belief are not stated, the main discovery was of Roman brick and masonry work which seemed to indicate a forum.

There was no doubt that the walls found were very solid and intended to be imposing. They did not appear to belong to a domestic house; they were far too large for this. The walls actually stretched all the way round the castle, which of course would not even have existed at the time that they were built. One possibility is that they represented an inner wall of defence, a much smaller fortified area within the main walls of the Roman city. The main argument against this is that it seemed clear that the inside surface of the walls had been plastered and painted a salmon pink. This is hardly the sort of homely touch which one would expect to find on a military barrier! It is, on the other hand, precisely the sort of thing one might see on a market place or forum.

MARCH 10TH

2012: Boxten Methodist Silver Band played on this day at the Essex town of Holland-on-Sea. Methodism has a very strong tradition in Colchester and the surrounding villages, with roots going back to the very beginning of the movement, when John Wesley himself visited the town many times during his travels.

The Boxten Methodist Silver Band began in 1898, although thirty years before that there was a wind band connected with the chapel. The present name of the band was fixed in 1938. At this time, the members of the band wore uniforms almost indistinguishable from those of the Salvation Army.

The one thing which all the members of the band have in common today is a love of this kind of music. Not all those who play in the band belong to the chapel, although the majority do. There are currently eleven cornets, four horns, four trombones, two euphoniums and various others in the band, although they are always on the lookout for new members. So enthusiastic are the members of the band that they have recently started a practice band for those who feel that they might wish to learn to play one of the instruments but currently lack the skill.

MARCH 11TH

1859: Lexden Methodists held a meeting this day to discuss their plans for building a chapel in Lexden, on the outskirts of Colchester. The Methodists have always had a strong following in Colchester; right back as far as the days when John Wesley, founder of the denomination, was a regular visitor to the town.

The year before the crucial meeting which gave the go-ahead to acquire land on which to build a chapel, the Methodists in Lexden had held a camp meeting. This was fine as a one-off, but they were determined to have a permanent base. Those taking part in these meetings, minutes of which survive, sound like characters from a novel by Thomas hardy; Brother Steggles, Brother Bugg, Isaac Dowman, Joshua Elsden. Brother Bloomfield and Brother Bugg were given permission to buy the land at Lexden needed for the chapel. There seemed to have been a thriving Methodist congregation at that time, because at the same meeting, Camp Meetings were planned for Fingringhoe, Brightlingsea, Kirby, Thorpe and Mile End.

They moved fast in those days, because the foundation stone of the new chapel was laid in September that year and the building was opened for worship by November! It is still in use today.

MARCH 12TH

1969: This is the day that Graham Coxon, lead guitarist of the band Blur, was born in Germany. His family returned to England when he was small, living first in Derbyshire. While he was still young, the family moved to Colchester, where Coxon grew up and went to school. When he was twelve, he met Damon Albarn at Stanway School, which they both attended.

The two of them later went to Goldsmith's College in London, where they met Alex James, who would also become a member of the band. They initially called the band Seymour, after the character Seymour Glass in the short stories by J.D. Salinger. The first gig by the new band was held only five miles from Colchester in the East Anglian Railway Museum. That same year, they were signed up by Food Records. One stipulation was that the name of the band should be changed and after a good deal of thought, they came up with Blur.

On June 13th 2009, Blur played their first comeback gig in the same location as their very first performance twenty years earlier – in the converted goods shed at the East Anglian Railway Museum.

MARCH 13TH

1971: This was the first open day and opportunity to ride in a steam train at the East Anglian Rail Museum, just outside Colchester. This open-air museum has its roots in the Stour Valley Railway Preservation Society, formed in 1968 to try and prevent a recently closed section of rail line from falling into a state of ruin. This led directly to the founding of the East Anglian Railway Museum some years later.

The museum is based at Chappel and Wakes Colne Station. For the railway enthusiast, this museum is something of a Mecca. In addition to the steam engines which haul passenger trains, there are also diesels and a replica Thomas the Tank Engine. There are engine sheds where dedicated hobbyists help to maintain and restore steam engines. The acquisition of new stock is a continuous and ongoing process. The museum is an enormously popular destination for families on days out during weekends and school holidays. The fascination of small boys for steam trains seems to be as strong as ever!

March 14th

1883: This was the day that Karl Marx died, leaving behind as his principle monument the massive work *Das Kapital*. This famously indigestible, some would say unreadable, masterpiece, has a curious connection to Colchester. Part of the book deals in exhaustive detail with specific historical examples of the theory of capitalist accumulation; into which theory readers should be grateful that we are not about to delve in detail! One of the instances which Marx cites in his book is that of a small Essex village during the Industrial Revolution.

Fingringhoe lies about five miles from the centre of Colchester, so close that one might almost regard it as a suburb of the city. Marx details and categorises the process whereby the villagers of Fingringhoe were deprived of the fruits of their labour by unscrupulous landowners and how the workers became poorer and the landowners richer as a direct result. Strange to think that the economic affairs of this obscure little village should have been pored over and scrutinised by subsequent generations and that world leaders such as Lenin, Stalin and Mao Tse Tung should have been obliged to read about life in rural Fingringhoe!

MARCH 15TH

1897: Albert Eliot Marshall was born in Elmstead Market, not far from Colchester, on this day. In 1915, he lied about his age and joined the Essex Yeomanry at the age of 17, so desperate was he to take part in the First World War. Nicknamed 'Smiler', Albert Marshall saw action at Loos and Cambrai. After the end of the war in 1918, he volunteered to serve in Ireland.

So far, there is nothing unusual about Albert Marshall's experiences; millions of British men served in the army during the First World War. However, Albert outlived almost all of them. He had been a cavalryman during the First World War, at a time when the use of horses was already something of an anachronism. He lived to the age of a 108, not dying until well into the twenty-first century. He was survived by one son, twelve grandchildren, twenty-four great-grandchildren and four great-great-grandchildren. He acquired his nickname as a result of an incident while training at Stanway, when he threw a snowball at a drill sergeant who had promised to give the young recruit something to smile about.

MARCH 16TH

1835: On this day reports were made to Parliament about the salaries and duties of prison chaplains in England and Wales. The information from Essex threw up one or two surprises. The chaplain at the Colchester House of Correction, Revd Morgan, was being paid £40 a year; not a bad wage for the time. His duties could hardly be described as onerous, because only two prisoners were being held at the prison, which was still in Colchester Castle. He was being paid considerably more than the average wage of a working man for holding one service at 1 p.m. on Sundays and a brief session of prayers on Thursdays.

It was clear that the chaplain was embarrassed when it came to light how little he was doing for the money which he received. In justification of his position, he pointed out that he had been employed by the prison since 1817, at which time there were far more prisoners and the work had involved a lot of pastoral visiting. At times, there were over thirty-four prisoners confined in the castle. New regulation brought in in 1823 had meant that Colchester Castle could no longer hold more than two or three prisoners. Then, as now, questions asked in Parliament could reveal much wasting of public funds.

MARCH 17TH

1821: The so-called Colchester Sphinx was discovered on this day during the digging of foundations for a new building. This Roman sculpture, a little less than 3 feet high, was probably part of a larger funerary monument. It is of a winged human figure, similar in some ways to an angel, holding a man's bearded head. It is made of French stone and probably dates from the first decades of the Roman occupation.

What is interesting about this statue is the way in which interpretations of it have changed over the years. One of those who was present when it was unearthed described it as being the, 'ancient figure of the Theban Sphinx, which here is represented as having already slain a victim of her wiles . . . she sits, as it were, in perfect serenity over the mangled remains of her unsuccessful opponent'. A hundred and fifty years later, an archaeologist calls the same sculpture, 'the peaceful symbol of death's riddle', going on to talk of the supposed victim as, 'one sleeping serenely in the care of his protectress'.

Those who wish to see the Colchester Sphinx for themselves and decide whether it depicts a bloodthirsty monster or guardian angel will find it on display in the museum in Colchester Castle.

MARCH 18TH

2005: The Mersea Island Brewery opened on this day. Alcoholic drink has been made on Mersea Island since the Roman occupation 2,000 years ago. The present vineyards are to be found in East Mersea, where the wine is also fermented. The vineyards are combined with a bed and breakfast holiday centre. In 2005, it was decided that the brewing of beer would sit well alongside the fermenting of wine and so a small brewery was opened. The opening ceremony was attended by members of the Campaign for Real Ale (CAMRA) and landlords of various local pubs. The ribbon was cut by Helen McDermott, an Anglia Television presenter. A café was opened at the same time.

The beers produced on Mersea were quickly found to be of a high quality, winning various awards. Without doubt, the most unusual beer of all was one called Island Oyster. This was brewed using, as the name suggests, oysters. Each cask of the ale has eight Mersea oysters added to it. It is rumoured, although not yet confirmed, that this particular beer has aphrodisiac qualities.

MARCH 19TH

1942: The air-raid sirens on Mersea Island were last sounded on this day during the Second World War. It was not quite the last time that they have ever been used; they were heard once more after the war as a flood warning. At the time of writing, it is thought that they will soon be dismantled, as it is impossible to obtain the spare parts necessary for their maintenance.

German bombers often flew over or past Mersea, on their way to bomb industrial or military targets inland. Despite having 2,000 troops stationed on the island though, it was never regarded by the Luftwaffe as a prime target. By 1942, the tide of the war had turned and it was allied bombers which were passing overhead on their way to bomb Germany. There are still a few remnants of the Second World War to be found if one knows where to look. During the fear of war which swept the country in 1938, the War Ministry ordered the parish council at West Mersea to built a concrete road above the beach. This survives to this day as Victoria Esplanade. The Two Sugars Café on the esplanade is situated above a huge ammunition store, which has now been sealed up.

MARCH 20TH

1997: On this day, the last part of Severalls Hospital closed forever. Severalls had been built as an asylum in 1910, opening three years later. Housing 2,000 residents with mental health problems, the hospital was designed on the 'Echelon Plan'. This meant that most buildings on the 300-acre site were linked by covered corridors, so that doctors and other staff did not need to walk outside in bad weather.

Severalls was essentially a village or small town, with everything needed for the patients being available within the grounds of the hospital. There was a church, concert hall; it even boasted its own mortuary. Some of the residents lived in the place for decades, eventually dying of old age with no hope of ever returning to the outside world.

Not only mentally ill people were detained at Severalls. As late as the 1950s, women who had been raped or had illegitimate babies could find themselves being committed to places like this by their families. Once there, they could be subjected to terrifying experimental treatments such as Electroconvulsive Therapy (ECT) and lobotomies.

As 'Care in the Community' ethos gained ground in the 1980s, most of Severalls' residents were moved out. A small geriatric unit remained, but by 1997, this too was surplus to requirements and closed down.

MARCH 21ST

1688: Augustin King, a highwayman, was hanged at Colchester on this day. Until the building of the railway lines in the 1830s and '40s, north Essex was a pretty remote location, served only by stagecoaches. Travellers in the late eighteenth century were always at risk of being accosted by highwaymen. The best way to deter robberies of this sort was thought in those days to be by the liberal use of the death penalty. Those convicted of highway robbery were almost invariably hanged after being caught and tried.

Not all highwaymen were thugs. Claude Duval was a famous example of the more gentlemanly highwayman. He came from an impoverished French family and his manners were always impeccable when stopping stagecoaches and depriving passengers of their money. Augustin King was another example of this breed. Incredibly, his father was a well known and respected vicar. King went to Cambridge University as a young man, but fell into debt. Robbing travellers on the London to Colchester road seemed to him a straightforward and uncomplicated way of raising money.

MARCH 22ND

1811: On this day, a bizarre incident occurred during a stagecoach journey from London to Norwich. It must be noted that while some passengers travelled inside the coaches, cheaper seats were also available on the top. On this particular journey, a man and his mother were travelling to Colchester. The mother, an elderly woman, was the only passenger actually inside the coach – all the others were travelling outside.

When the stagecoach reached the Essex village of Ingatestone, where the horses were changed, it was discovered that the woman inside the coach had died. The driver naturally assumed that the woman's son would wish to have his mother's body taken off and arrangements made for a more suitable mode of transport to Colchester. He, however, was determined to continue the journey, aiming to make any necessary arrangements once they reached Colchester. Reluctantly, the driver agreed. When the coach reached Chelmsford, two women who had booked 'inside' tickets from there to Colchester, tried to board the coach. The driver quietly explained what had happened and that the only 'inside' passenger was sitting in the coach, dead. The two women though were not at all discouraged by this and insisted on travelling anyway. They accordingly spent the whole journey from Chelmsford to Colchester sitting opposite a corpse.

MARCH 23RD

1922: On this day, Robert Whitcombe, Bishop of Colchester, died. Although he took holy orders at Oxford University, Whitcombe's early career was that of schoolmaster. He taught at Wellington College and Eton until the age of 37. It was not until 1899 that he first took up a post as Rector at Hardwick in Buckinghamshire. He was later appointed vicar of Romford. In 1909, he became the Bishop of Colchester, taking over from Henry Johnson, who had died the previous year.

The post of Bishop of Colchester was originally created during the Reformation in 1534. Before the First World War, it was hoped by many that Colchester would become the seat of the Church of England Diocese in Essex. Instead, Chelmsford, the county town, was chosen. Since that time, the Suffragen bishops of Colchester have been demoted somewhat in authority. They are now under the jurisdiction of the Bishop of Chelmsford.

March 24th

1992: The Wharf at the upstream shipyard in Wivenhoe closed for good on this day. Wivenhoe has a history of shipbuilding dating back to the reign of Elizabeth I. In 1575, one Richard Quykeskey rented a shipyard upstream of the quay and for the next four centuries, boat building would be central to the economy of Wivenhoe.

The port at Wivenhoe was extremely busy at one time. Cloth made in Colchester was exported via Wivenhoe, oysters and fish landed and taken inshore, boats built and, in addition to commercial shipping, the town began to become important for the sport of sailing. At the end of the nineteenth century a dry dock was constructed; the only one between London and Lowestoft. This was used for the construction of iron-clad ships which were built and then dismantled, being sent to the buyers in kit form. An example of a ship of this sort is still operating to this day – the pleasure steamer *Tern* still plies Lake Windemere.

In 1986, James W. Cook & Co. Ltd, the downstream shipyard which was also the town's largest employer, closed. The upstream wharf closed six years later, bringing this chapter in Wivenhoe's story to a close.

MARCH 25TH

2004: The *Evening Gazette* reported on this day that £50,000 was to be spent by the council on repairing the Roman city wall in Colchester. The wall surrounding the centre of Colchester, which marks the extent of the ancient Roman city, stretches for three kilometres and is almost completely intact in places. Unfortunately, although Colchester Council definitely owns large sections of the wall, the ownership of other parts is debatable. For example, some of the wall backs onto the gardens of houses and it is far from clear whether the wall is inside or outside their property; or even whether it actually marks the boundary.

The city wall in Colchester is both a Scheduled Ancient Monument and also Grade I listed. Some of it is astonishingly well preserved, with the ragstone blocks and tile courses looking as though they could easily be good for another 2,000 years. It runs through car parks and private gardens, snakes between buildings and may be seen peeping coyly from beneath modern developments.

MARCH 26TH

1926: Edmund John Fowler VC died on this day. He was born in Ireland and awarded the Victoria Cross at the age of 18 for his actions during the Zulu War of 1879.

On March 28th 1879, Fowler was at the Zlobane Mountain in South Africa. Accompanied by two officers – a captain and a lieutenant – they were supposed to clear the enemy from a cave which was in a commanding position. The path leading to the cave was so narrow that it was only possible to advance in single file. The captain led the way and, as soon as he arrived at the mouth of the cave, he was shot dead. Fowler and the lieutenant sprang at the Zulus occupying the cave and, in a fierce fight, managed to kill them all.

Edmund Fowler stayed in the army for many years, eventually rising to the rank of Colour-Sergeant. On leaving the army, he became the landlord of the Live and Let Live public house in Stanway Street in Colchester. He was a popular host and ran the pub until his death at the age of 65. He is buried in Colchester.

MARCH 27TH

1908: The famous pianist Alberto Semprini was born on this day. During the 1950s, '60s and '70s, he was as well know in this country as Liberace was in America. In 1957, the BBC began broadcasting a programme which Semprini compered; called *Semprini Serenade*. Semprini introduced the programme, in which he played a selection of light classical music, with the words 'Old ones, new ones, loved ones, neglected ones'. It ran until the early 1980s.

For most of the years that he was a radio star, Semprini lived on a houseboat called *L'Esperance*, which was moored at West Mersea. Passers-by would stop at the gangplank to listen to the pianist practicing. He also rehearsed on a grand piano in the back of a shop in Barfield Road.

Semprini's style, perfectly suited to the radio, never really caught on with television audiences and when *Semprini Serenade* ended in 1982, he sank into obscurity, dying eight years later in 1990.

MARCH 28TH

1794: On this day Joseph Herrick was born in Wolverhampton. His father was a jeweller, but young Joseph was very religious and became a Sunday school teacher. At the age of 20, he was appointed as pastor to a nonconformist chapel in St Helen's Lane, Colchester. From the beginning, he was a controversial preacher. For one thing, he seemed to exercise a hypnotic influence upon female members of the congregation, to such an extent that a number of men banded together and prevented their daughters and wives from attending the chapel.

The situation between Joseph Herrick and his flock became so tense that the trustees began publishing pamphlets denouncing their young pastor. In 1816, there occurred a most extraordinary incident, when some of the male members of the congregation removed the roof of the chapel, thus making it impossible for Herrick to lead services there. He responded by holding meetings in his back garden.

He may have had opponents, but Joseph Herrick also had many supporters. A new chapel was built, the Stockwell chapel, and it opened in 1817. It was soon extended so that it could seat over a thousand and Joseph Herrick continued to preach in Colchester for almost fifty years, until his death in 1865.

MARCH 29TH

1843: Colchester's main railway station opened on this day. It is not particularly convenient for the town centre and so is known locally as Colchester North, to distinguish it from the more centrally located Colchester Town station, which was built a little over twenty years later. Colchester North is on the main line from Liverpool Street Station in London, whereas Colchester Town is on a minor route connecting Colchester with Clacton.

The main Colchester station was built during the great railway boom of the 1840s. The aim was speed at that time, with various different companies competing frantically to see who could be the first to reach different districts. Colchester North was built where it is in order to avoid some tricky engineering works which would have entailed two river crossings. The problem was that bringing it into the centre of the town would have entailed making a detour across the River Colne. When first it opened, horse-drawn wagons took passengers from the station into the town itself. The railway company tried to promote development around their new station; if the railway could not come to the town, perhaps they could persuade the town to come to the railway!

Colchester North is still a very popular and busy station, even in these days of almost universal ownership of cars. Over four million passengers use the station each year.

MARCH 30TH

2001: On this day, Youth Culture Limited was registered as a charity. Based in the Saxon church of Holy Trinity, in which it operates a café, the charity is seeking to renovate and restore the church.

Holy Trinity is the oldest building in Colchester and contains two very rare architectural features. One of these is a pointed arch. The Saxons never really mastered the technique of constructing arches and so sometimes resorted simply to placing two slabs leaning together and forming a pointed structure above a window or door. The other part of this old church worth noting is the tower. This was built in about 1020, half a century before the Norman invasion, and, as such, is one of only a handful of Saxon church towers to be found in Britain.

These days, the church no longer holds services but acts as a base for Youth Culture Limited, which also calls itself CO1. Many youth centre activities take place in the old church and the café is a popular place for shoppers of all ages.

MARCH 31ST

2007: On this day, the end of the financial year, the Home Office releases various statistics relating to crime and the frequency of different offences in places around the country. Colchester's figures always compare favourably with the rest of Britain.

Colchester had at that time a population of 177,000, living in 73,000 households. Nationally, an average of 9.7 people per thousand suffer from burglaries. In Colchester, the figure is only 6.4. This means that there is roughly a 33 per cent less chance of having your house broken into if you live in Colchester; as opposed to the rest of the country. The figures for vandalism and criminal damage are about the same in the town as they are elsewhere, but hearteningly, drug-related offences are half of what they are in the country as a whole.

As a matter of fact, the rates for every single type of offence are lower in Colchester than they are generally throughout the country. In some cases, the difference is very great. Your chances of being mugged on the streets of Colchester are about a third of what they are in the rest of the country.

APRIL 1ST

1974: Colchester Borough was formed on this day. It was created by amalgamating the former borough of Colchester, which covered only the town itself, with the boroughs of West Mersea, Wivenhoe and Lexden. The change in status at that time was not one connected solely with Colchester. It was a direct result of the 1972 Local Authorities Act, which sought to rationalise the structure of local authorities. The situation with county boroughs, areas with large populations which were not under the jurisdiction of the County Council, had become increasingly complicated and unworkable.

The current arrangement is that Colchester Borough is responsible for the provision of a range of local services, but its powers are subordinate in many cases to those of Essex County Council. The old county boroughs have in a sense crept back into existence with the introduction of Unitary Authorities. Thurrock and Southend, for example, are completely independent of the County Council and run their own local affairs more or less autonomously. This is not the case with Colchester.

APRIL 2ND

2012: On this day, Colchester's new magistrates' court was opened on time and within budget. It is surely a sign of the times that an announcement that a public building should be ready when planned and cost no more than was initially thought, should rate a special newspaper story! The *Essex County Standard*, though, certainly thought such an event newsworthy when it covered the story.

The new complex at St Botolph's Circus overlooks what will eventually become a town square. The futuristic appearance of the building, which houses four separate courtrooms, as well as a youth court and family facility, was dubbed 'The Marmite Building'. The reasons for this nomenclature are wholly obscure.

One person who was not happy with the new court was local MP Sir Bob Russell, who said, 'To my mind the building is ugly, out of scale and out of keeping'. He went on to claim that Colchester boasted better looking and more attractive multi-storey car parks than the new court building. Sir Bob called for the councillors who had voted for the new court's design to be named and shamed.

APRIL 3RD

1943: Edna Jean Coe died on this day and despite the fact that she was a civilian, her name is to be found on the war memorial at Wivenhoe. The explanation for this is an intriguing one. In 1942, Jean, as everyone knew her, was a 17-year-old pupil at Colchester High School for Girls. She hoped to train as a nurse, but a recruiting team from the Ministry of Supply visited the school and appealed for recruits to work testing chemicals at the Royal Ordnance Factory in Staffordshire. Jean volunteered and put her nursing studies to one side.

Her job at the factory entailed taking samples of newly manufactured explosives from various magazines at the factory and carrying them to a laboratory to be analysed and quality checked. On April 3rd 1943, one of the batches proved to be faulty and the entire magazine exploded as Jean collected the sample. She died three hours later.

Wivenhoe Parish Council decided that although she had been a civilian, Jean Coe had given her life for the war effort in just the same way that a soldier might do and so decided that her name should be included in the list of those who had fallen in action.

April 4th

1850: Arthur Othniel Stopes was born on this day. He was managing director of the Colchester Brewing Company, which at one time owned fifty-eight of the public houses in Colchester. It also owned 261 pubs in the rest of Essex, Norfolk and Suffolk. The Colchester Brewing Company had been formed in the nineteenth century by the amalgamation of a number of smaller companies. The Eye Brewing Company, for example, had merged with Falcon Breweries to form the Norfolk and Suffolk Brewing Company. C. Stopes & Sons of Colchester then combined with them to form the Colchester Brewing Company.

The old headquarters of the Colchester Brewing Company still stands on East Hill in Colchester. It is a prefect example of Victorian industrial architecture; it could easily be part of a set for Charles Dickens' *Hard Times*. It is a marvellously solid and uncompromising building; designed to make a statement about the company which had it built. Stopes is mentioned on the foundation stone.

The Colchester Brewing Company was itself taken over by another Essex company in 1925, when Ind Coope of Romford bought them up. The name ended completely in 1959.

APRIL 5TH

1771: The owners of the *Chelmsford and Colchester Chronicle or Essex Weekly Advertiser* were declared bankrupt on this day. A number of local newspapers have been set up over the years to cover events in Colchester, of which this was only one. The new owners of the *Chelmsford and Colchester Chronicle or Essex Weekly Advertiser* decided to streamline the paper once they had taken it over. The title was so unwieldy, even for those days, that it had to be cut down to manageable size. It was re-launched as the *Chelmsford Chronicle*. A few years later, the name was changed to the *Essex County Chronicle*, in an attempt to make it sound a little less parochial and to appeal to a readership outside Chelmsford. From 1864 to 1871, a Colchester edition of this newspaper was published, focusing upon Colchester rather than Chelmsford.

Other local newspapers dealing exclusively or primarily with Colchester news were the *Colchester Gazette* and the *Colchester Courier*, started in 1814 and 1829 respectively. The two papers subsequently amalgamated and then stopped publication entirely in 1844. The *Colchester Gazette* was revived in 1877 with somewhat more success and continued publication under this name until 1970.

April 6th

1929: The *Essex County Standard* reported on this day the death of Charles Edwin Benham. Charles Benham was a well-known journalist, who was born in Colchester on April 15th 1860. He attended the Royal Colchester Grammar School. His family owned the *Essex County Standard*, a local newspaper which concentrated upon news from Colchester and the surrounding villages. From 1892 until his death in 1929, Charles Benham edited this newspaper jointly with his brother William.

Charles Benham was something more than a provincial newspaper editor. He was also a keen amateur scientist who regularly contributed articles to the prestigious magazine *Nature*. He was interested in physics and botany, also writing for the *Journal of Botany*. As if all this were not enough, he was a talented artist as well, especially in the medium of watercolours. Like his brother, William Gurney Benham, who in 1933 was appointed High Steward of Colchester, Charles Benham was a JP.

On his death, an obituary of Benham appeared in *Nature*, which described him as 'a representative of the type of scientific amateur of which British science has reason to be proud'. He is chiefly remembered today for his invention of the 'Benham's Top'; a disc of black and white lines which, when spun, creates the illusion of vivid colours.

APRIL 7TH

2007: A group of 'urban explorers' reported that they had mounted an expedition to St Albright's Hospital on this day. Urban explorers visit derelict, abandoned or off-limits sites and take photographs of them. Sometimes they take little souvenirs as well. Colchester has a few places which attract devotees of this pastime. St Albright's is a listed building in Stanway, just outside Colchester, which was once a workhouse. It became a hospital in the twentieth century, but is now derelict. It has, since 1982, enjoyed Grade II listed status.

The name of the website where the report on the visit to St Albright's is archived is quite revealing; it is called *28 Days Later*. This was, of course, the title of a post-apocalyptic film about a world infested with flesh-eating zombies.

Psychiatric hospitals seem to have a fascination for urban explorers; Severalls Hospital is another popular haunt. Industrial architecture also attracts them. A number of expeditions have been made to the top of the Jumbo water tower under the cover of darkness. Climbing this local landmark is technically trespassing, which is why such activities take place at night.

APRIL 8TH

2007: The last ever service in Colchester's Garrison Church, otherwise known as the Camp Church, was held on this day. This wooden building dates from the Crimean War of 1854-1856 and was the first permanent building of what would become Colchester Garrison.

The old white-painted church is an early example of a pre-fabricated building; the whole thing being made of pine planks held together with foot-long iron bolts. The company which produced the Garrison Church also made pre-fabricated wooden hospitals of the type Florence Nightingale worked during the Crimean War in the same system. A refurbishment in 1988 found that the place was in a remarkably good state of preservation for a structure which had originally been intended as temporary.

There was some anxiety when the garrison site was being developed about the future of the church. For a time, it looked as though it might be demolished. In November 2008 though, the Garrison Church was taken over by, and has since been run by, the Russian Orthodox Church. Today it is dedicated to St John the Wonderworker.

APRIL 9TH

1677: This is the day that a 'Monstrous Whale' became stranded on the banks of the River Colne where it flows through Colchester. It was, according to contemporary accounts, 42 feet long and was killed by the people in the town. The event was so impressive that a pamphlet was published about it later that year, with the imposing title 'Wonders from the Deep, or a true and exact account and description of the monstrous whale lately taken near Colchester, being 2 and 40 feet in length and of bigness proportionable, with the manner of its coming and being killed on Thursday, April 9th, being so rare and strange a sight that multitudes of people from all parts daily go to see it as thick as a market or fair'!

Whales which lost their way and ended up in rivers far from the sea exercised a great fascination for people in the seventeenth century. Sadly, there is no way now of knowing just what sort of whale this might have been.

Lest we laugh at an age where a stranded whale attracted crowds of gawping sightseers, let us remember that precisely the same thing happened in the heart of London a few years ago. In 2006, a northern bottlenose whale swam up the Thames as far as Battersea. Just as in 1677, this was, 'so rare and strange a sight that multitudes of people from all parts' descended on the area to stand and stare.

April 10th

1656: We are so used today to our freedom to worship in whatever way seems best to us, that it is easy to forget that at one time those who wouldn't conform to the traditional churches were persecuted. In the summer of 1655, a 19-year-old youth called James Parnell arrived in Colchester. He was a devout Quaker and wished to share his faith with others. He preached at St Nicholas' Church and then moved on to Coggeshall. Exactly what happened in the church there when he tried to explain his beliefs is unclear, but the upshot was that he was arrested for blasphemy and lodged in Colchester Castle, then being used as a prison, to await trial.

Although acquitted of the main charge, he was fined £40 for 'brawling'. He refused to pay and was returned to his cell in the castle. The jailer, Nicholas Roberts, was famous for being a cruel and vindictive man. Among other things, he made Parnell climb a rope in order to get his food. This resulted in a fall and on April 10th 1656, James Parnell died. A plaque in Colchester Castle marks the room which was his cell. Another plaque in Colchester's Quaker Meeting House also commemorates this brave man.

APRIL 11TH

1884: Thomas Davids died on this day. He was an evangelical young Welsh nonconformist minister who took over Colchester's Lions Walk Chapel in 1841. At that time, religious feelings ran a good deal more strongly than they do today and Revd Davids arrival caused the chapel's congregation to split; with half leaving to found a new church of their own. Thomas Davids stuck at it though and became one of the most popular and successful ministers in the whole of Colchester.

The Lions Walk Sunday school particularly flourished under the young minister, boasting at its height over a thousand pupils. Reverend Davids remained the pastor at Lions Walk for thirty-four years, overseeing the demolition of the old building and its replacement with an altogether grander gothic structure with a tall spire, looking more like a High Anglican or Catholic church than a nonconformist chapel. It was nicknamed St David's Cathedral. Eleven days after Thomas Davids' death, the great Colchester earthquake struck and the topmost part of the Lions Walk spire was brought crashing down. Some saw this as the Lord's disapproval in action . . .

April 12th

1996: Colchester Archaeological Trust held a watching brief for some building work which began on this day in Straight Road, Lexden. Their interest was in details of the dyke system, which were revealed as the builders excavated the site.

A curious feature of the Celtic town of Camulodunum, which once stood where Colchester is today, is that it had no defensive walls. The ancient Britons relied heavily upon the use of chariots in warfare – long after their use had been abandoned in mainland Europe. When Julius Caesar came to Britain in 55 BC and again in 54 BC, he found that chariots were very much in evidence. The easiest way to protect a settlement from an assault by chariots is simply to dig ditches and raise up ridges of earth around your home. If such structures are created at sufficient distance, then an enemy army will be deterred.

All around ancient Colchester was a vast network of such ditches and banks, which have become known as dykes. A curious modern counterpart to this type of defensive earthwork are the ditches and heaped earth which encircle some areas of open land where it is supposed that travellers might try to enter. In appearance, these are identical, albeit on a smaller scale, to the dykes around Colchester.

APRIL 13TH

1824: Jane Taylor died on this day. She wrote one of the most famous nursery rhymes in the English language; Twinkle, Twinkle, Little Star. Although she was born in London, Jane and her family later moved to Colchester and it was while she living there that she wrote the jingle for which she is most widely known. Her father was an engraver from Ongar, also in Essex, who later became a nonconformist minister.

Jane and her sister, Ann, wrote a good deal of poetry. In 1804, they published *Original Poems for Infant Minds by Several Young Persons.* The two main 'young persons' being Jane and her sister. They later produced another volume of *Original Poems for Infant Minds* and then in 1806, a third, entitled *Rhymes for the Nursery.* It was here that Twinkle, Twinkle first appeared, under the title, 'The Star'.

Twinkle, Twinkle, Little Star is hardly ever credited with the author's name. It has been adapted, changed and parodied so much that few people seem to be aware that it was actually written by one person. It is invariably sung to the tune of an old melody by Mozart; *Ah! vous dirai-je, Maman.* Jane Taylor herself died of cancer at the age of 40 and is today remembered only for this one nursery rhyme.

APRIL 14TH

1917: On this day, Richard Wasey Chopping was born in Colchester. The name Richard Chopping might not mean much to people today, but fifty years ago he was an artist whose works were instantly recognisable by millions of people throughout the world. You would not have gone to an art gallery though to see his paintings.

Chopping was an illustrator, specialising in book jackets. His most famous commissions and the ones which are instantly recognisable are the covers of Ian Fleming's James Bond books, the first of which was the artwork for *From Russia with Love*, in 1957. Chopping painted in the *trompe l'oeil* style; ultra realistic and making the objects look almost three-dimensional. For the first of the dust jackets which he produced for the James Bond books, for instance, he painted a .38 revolver lying on top of a rose.

Seventeen years after Ian Fleming's death brought an end to the James Bond books, another author was found who agreed to revive the series. Richard Chopping did the cover for the first of these books; *Licence Renewed* by John Gardner. It was an update of his first James Bond cover, only this time showing an automatic pistol rather than a revolver. Richard Chopping died in 2008.

April 15th

1905: Rear Admiral John Lee-Barber was born on this day. He lived in Wivenhoe for the last fourteen years of his life. Rear-Admiral Lee-Barber was perhaps the most aggressive destroyer commander of the Second World War. He joined the navy as a cadet in 1919, when he was only 14. He gained his first command in 1937, the ship was HMS *Witch*. This was followed by *Ardent* and then *Griffin* in 1939. He carried out some daring patrols in the North Sea during the Norwegian Campaign and in 1940 he helped to evacuate Polish soldiers from France. For this action he was later awarded the Polish Cross of Valour. In the same year he received the Distinguished Service Order (DSO) for his patrols in the English Channel at a time when many people expected a German invasion.

In 1943, Lee-Barber was given command of HMS *Opportune*. He took part in the pursuit of the *Scharnhorst*, being mentioned in despatches when his ship managed to hit the German cruiser with two torpedoes. He retired in 1959, at which time he was appointed CBE. In 1981, at the age of 76, he moved to Wivenhoe, living in Ferry House on the Quay until his death at the age of 90.

APRIL 16TH

1636: Richard Farnham from Colchester was examined for heresy on this day – which was at that time a capital crime. Farnham was a weaver in Colchester, who, in 1636, decided that he was a prophet with a message from God. He travelled to London with his divine message and teamed up with another weaver there called John Bull, who also thought that he was inspired by God. Before going to London, Farnham had contracted a bigamous marriage, which he later justified on scriptural grounds. He and his fellow prophet were soon arrested.

While being held at Newgate Prison, Richard Farnham petitioned the Archbishop of Canterbury, William Laud, for his release. He rather tactlessly described himself in his letters to the Archbishop as 'a prophet of the most high God'. One of the specific accusations made against him was that he had claimed to be either Christ or Elijah. He certainly prophesied that on his death he would rise again, and, after five years of being held variously in Newgate, Bridewell and the Bethlehem lunatic asylum, he was able to put this particular claim to the test. In 1641, he died of plague and several of his disciples waited expectantly for his resurrection. They were to be disappointed.

APRIL 17TH

1776: On this day, John Howard, the famous prison reformer, visited Colchester lock-up and described the conditions he found there, the results of which were published in a book called *The State of the Prisons in England and Wales*:

> The castle was formerly the County Gaol. That part of it which is now the Bridewell has first, the room for women, with a fireplace; on one side a room for men, with a window; on another side two rooms for men, at a right angle with the former; a window at the farthermost. The partitions are iron grated for light and air, from the window and each end of the right angle-Court-yard little used by prisoners. No water; no employment; allowance 3d a day; straw £2 a year. Keeper's Salary £30.

It sounds a grim enough existence and Howard regarded the conditions at Colchester at this time as being unfit for any human. There is one positive note though, and that is that the prison seemed hardly ever to be used. In 1774, there was only one prisoner when an inspection was made and, two years later, there were only three.

APRIL 18TH

1996: The *Independent* reported on this day that Colchester's 'Glasshouse' was to be used to house thirty-two young offenders in a special civilian wing. The Military Corrective Training Centre, to give the 'glasshouse' its full and correct name, has been a well-known feature of Colchester for many decades. It was the place where those in the armed forces who committed serious offences against military discipline could be sent.

According to Ann Widdecombe, Minister of State for the Home Office, the young detainees would not be subject to military law while at Colchester, but would certainly face a harsher regime than those in civilian prisons. Even the right to watch television would have to be earned in stages. The day for these young men would begin with two and a half hours of physical exercise and they would also be drilled in army fashion. Allowances would, however, be made for the fact that they were likely to be less physically fit than members of the armed forces held at Colchester.

Sending young offenders to Colchester glasshouse was part of a pilot project for a high intensity young offenders training programme, aimed to reduce the re-offending rate for young people, which stood at 70 per cent.

APRIL 19TH

2011: On this date a copy of the *Colchester Evening News* appeared in an episode of *Dr Who*.

Colchester was the setting for two episodes of the BBC's science fiction series. In this one, the Doctor discovers that electrical disturbances are linked to various mysterious disappearances in the town. He works in the toy section of a department store and it is when he visits the premises after closing time that the nature of the problem is revealed to him: it is none other than his old enemies, the Cybermen.

As part of the plot, the Doctor, played by Matt Smith, hands the character playing Craig a newspaper. The bold heading is 'Evening News', in large black letters, but somebody who took the trouble to record the episode and then enlarge the newspaper found that the word 'Colchester' is also clearly visible, printed in red, along with the date, April 19th 2011.

It is rare for *Dr Who*, dealing as it does with travels in time and space, to allow anybody to pinpoint the precise date and place that the action takes place. The only other occasions when this has happened have been when the programme features some well-known historical event.

April 20th

1893: The Royal Yacht *Britannia* was launched on this day. Not of course the Royal Yacht *Britannia* which we remember from the 1960s and '70s, but an altogether earlier version. In 1891, Germany's Kaiser Wilhelm took delivery of a racing cutter called *Thistle*. She had been designed by George Lennox Watson and the Prince of Wales, soon to be King Edward VII, was so impressed that he commissioned the same man to design a yacht for him.

His Royal Highness' yacht, *Britannia*, was amazingly successful, winning thirty-three of the forty or so races in which she competed in her first year. On Edward VII's death, his son, George, had the *Britannia* refitted. Captain Albert Turner of Wivenhoe was her new skipper and he captained her to many successes during the 1920s. She was the oldest yacht in many of these races, but even so, Turner managed to beat the most up-to-date and modern boats against which he was competing. The *Britannia* won a total of 239 races.

It was George V's wish that the *Britannia* should follow him to his grave and after his death in 1936, she was towed out into the water around the Isle of Wight and sunk.

APRIL 21ST

1945: The last combat mission was flown from Boxted air base on this day. RAF Boxted, named after the nearby village, was four miles from Colchester and it was constructed in 1943 for the use of the US Air Force. East Anglia was the ideal location for the American bombers which pounded Germany in the later years of the Second World War. Boxted, whose USAAF code was BX, had three concrete runways set at 60 degree angles to each other, thus forming an equilateral triangle.

In addition to bombers, a number of fighter groups were also based at Boxted, where they flew sorties to accompany bombers and then, after the invasion of Europe, to provide ground cover for allied troops. The last sortie was flown just over a fortnight before the war ended on May 7th 1945.

After the war, the RAF Fighter Command took over Boxted and used it as a test base for their new jet fighters. At one time it was planned that Boxted should remain an RAF base in the post-war years, but there was a problem. The approach to the main runway lay over Colchester and although the risk and disturbance of having a stream of military aircraft flying over a major population centre could be justified during wartime, it was felt that different considerations applied in times of peace. The base closed on August 9th 1947.

APRIL 22ND

1884: Earthquakes are mercifully rare in this country, which made the one which struck Colchester on April 22nd 1884 all the more shocking. Its epicentre was the village of Wivenhoe, a few miles west of Colchester and, although it lasted only twenty seconds at 9.18 a.m., the tremors were felt as far away as France and Belgium. It measured 4.6 on the Richter Scale and was the most severe earth tremor to affect Britain in centuries.

In all, well over a thousand building were damaged, including almost every house in Wivenhoe itself. Chimneys were brought down as far away as Ipswich in Suffolk. According to *The Times*, many people were made homeless, but there is some confusion as to whether there were any fatalities. *The Times* reported the death of a child in Rowhedge as a result of the earthquake, and other contemporary accounts suggest that between three and five people were killed.

Tsunamis are another natural event with which we in this country are unfamiliar and yet the 1884 earthquake triggered one off the Essex coast. Many small boats were capsized and some lost altogether. There have been other earthquakes in this area, both before and since, but none as powerful as that of 1884.

APRIL 23RD

1828: This day saw William Corder, responsible for the so-called 'Red Barn Murder', lodging overnight at the George Inn in Colchester. Corder had seduced a woman called Maria Marten, who became pregnant. He himself was a pretty well-to-do young farmer's son, but she was the daughter of the local mole catcher. When Maria pressed him to marry her, Corder lured her to a barn on his father's land – the infamous 'Red Barn' – and then plunged a sword through her eye and into her brain. He then buried her in the barn. When the body was discovered, the jury at the inquest brought in a verdict of murder by William Corder. He was traced to London, where he was arrested.

Corder was brought back to Suffolk, where the murder had been committed. He and his escort reached Colchester on the evening of April 23rd and decided to break their journey there. An attempt was made to lodge the prisoner in Colchester Gaol for the night, but because there was no warrant, the governor refused to admit him. Instead, he was kept under guard at the George Inn. One of his wrists was tied to the bedpost for extra security. After his trial in Bury St Edmunds, William Corder was condemned to death and hanged in that town on August 11th 1828.

APRIL 24TH

1731: On this day the writer Daniel Defoe died. Although most famous as the author of *Robinson Crusoe* – generally accepted as the first English novel – Defoe also wrote a detailed portrait of England during the late seventeenth and early eighteenth centuries. *A Tour Through England* contains a good deal of information about Colchester. For example, Defoe mentions that during the great plague of 1665, 5,259 people died. This was, as Defoe writes, 'more in proportion than any of its neighbours, or than the city of London'.

In 1722, Daniel Defoe leased an old house called Tubswick, which was on the edge of the village of Mile End. Mile End or Myland, as it is also known, is now a suburb of Colchester. While living there, Defoe wrote his other masterpiece, *Moll Flanders*. The novel is partly set in Essex and Mile End village is mentioned in the text. According to Defoe in *A Tour Through England*, at the time that he was living there, Colchester had about 40,000 inhabitants, including those living in nearby villages.

In 2010, the house where Defoe once lived came within a whisker of being demolished. It had been gutted by a fire in 2009 and an application had been made to allow the Grade II listed building to be knocked down and housing built on the site. At the last minute, the application was withdrawn.

APRIL 25TH

2009: The Annual General Meeting of the Colchester Deaf Club took place on this day. In an era of stifling political correctness, it is more than a little refreshing to see a 'Deaf Club', rather than one for the 'hearing impaired'.

Reading the accounts on their website though of bingo for the deaf conjures up images of an increasingly despairing bingo caller, desperately trying to alert the players to the fact that the next number is eighty-eight or whatever! Doubtless there are ways around this difficulty.

Colchester's deaf community seem to be pretty well served in leisure activities. Intriguingly, there is even a Colchester Deaf Football Club. Most of us perhaps imagine football to be an almost entirely visual and physical game. Of course, there will be occasional shouts of 'Over here Jim!' and 'This way Jack!', but surely in the main the lack of acute hearing would not greatly hinder one in playing with those with better hearing. Even more odd is the fact that this football club is not restricted to deaf people, but is open to all. Surely in such a case it would cease to be a Deaf Football Club?

APRIL 26TH

1575: Marie de Medici was born on this day. Her visit to Essex in 1638, when she entered Colchester in state, was by all accounts an exceptionally grand affair.

Marie de Medici was, as her name suggests, Italian and in 1600 she married King Henri IV of France. Her children became variously Queen of Spain, King of France and Queen of England. The latter happened in 1625, when Henrietta Marie, her third daughter, married Charles I of England.

After the death of her husband, the King of France, Marie de Medici ruled for a time as regent, before being forced into exile by Cardinal Richelieu. Even in exile, however, the former queen was treated with incredible deference wherever she went. A visit to Amsterdam in 1638 was marked by the most spectacular water pageants. Flushed with success, she then decided to pay her son-in-law in London a visit.

Marie de Medici landed at Harwich to great adulation. Contemporary accounts suggest that she was feted wherever she went in the country. Her entry to Colchester was accompanied by music and fireworks, which had the effect that, 'those of the most melancholy disposition changed their humour, in order to join in the general rejoicing'. The streets were apparently lined with admiring crowds wherever she went in the town.

APRIL 27TH

1697: Jeremy Spurgin, clockmaker, was admitted as a burgess of Colchester on this day. This formality was necessary in order for him to undertake his trade in the town.

Colchester was something of a centre for the making of watches and clocks in the seventeenth and eighteenth centuries. Although he died at the early age of 33, Spurgin made a name for himself in the field. His former premises are still standing at 94 High Street. Curiously enough, and it cannot have been entirely coincidental, the same building was later occupied by John Smorthwaite, another well-known clockmaker in the town. Next door was the shop of Nathaniel Hedge, Smorthwaite's apprentice, who also went on to become a famous clockmaker in his own right.

Spurgin was from a Quaker family and showed an early aptitude for mechanical matters. In the Hollytrees Museum in Castle Park is a particularly fine example of his work; an early long case clock, what was once called a 'grandfather' clock. Spurgin completed it in 1698, less than a year before his death. It is one of the oldest long case clocks in the whole country.

APRIL 28TH

1556: On this day, six men were burned at the stake in Colchester for not subscribing fully to the tenets of the Catholic Church. Under Queen Mary, daughter of Henry VIII, determined efforts were made to roll back the Reformation which her father had begun. Colchester was something of a centre for religious persecution at that time, since the citizens were very quick to take to the idea of Protestantism during Henry's reign.

The six who were burned alive on April 28th are named on a memorial in St Peter's Church in Colchester as Christopher Lyster, John Mace, John Spencer, Simon Joyne, Richard Nichols and John Hamond. The memorial lists by name twenty-three others who died for their beliefs, roughly half of whom were women.

There is some indication that Essex in general and Colchester in particular were seen as hotbeds of rebellion against the Catholic faith. Most of those who died for their religious beliefs in this way were ordinary people who felt strongly enough that they were prepared to suffer the most hideous death imaginable rather than compromise their beliefs.

APRIL 29TH

2001: This was the day of the census, which provided a snapshot of Colchester soon after the beginning of the new millennium. The population of the borough was revealed to be 155,794 people – almost 12 per cent of the total population of Essex. 96.18 per cent of residents were white. The highest concentration of ethnic minorities was found around the ward of Wivenhoe Cross, where minorities made up 17 per cent of the population. The explanation for this is simple; it is the location of Essex University's campus, which has many overseas students in residence.

The average number of residents per household in the borough was 2.37; almost precisely the national average, which was found to be 2.36. Unemployment in Colchester was lower than average; 3.41 per cent, as opposed to 5 per cent for the country as a whole. A quarter of 16 to 74 year olds had no qualifications of any kind. The part of the borough with the lowest percentage of adults without qualifications was Wivenhoe Cross, with only 11.28 per cent of those living in this district having no qualifications. Hardly surprising that an area with many students should turn out to have fewer people without qualifications.

APRIL 30TH

2008: On this day the Phoenix Players from West Mersea were giving a dramatised performance of Dylan Thomas' *Under Milk Wood* in, of all unlikely places, the Waterford Institute of Technology in the Republic of Ireland. Just how this group from the island of Mersea ended up doing such an archetypal Welsh item is something of a mystery.

To begin with, the Phoenix Players seem to be a pretty shadowy bunch, with no presence at all on the internet. There are mentions of places where they have appeared, but no website nor any other information about how to contact them or where they are based; other than the fact that they are from West Mersea. Their production of *Under Milk Wood* must be up to scratch, because almost exactly a year after they were doing it in County Waterford, they were putting on the same show for the Chelmsford and District Welsh Society, who might presumably be expected to know a thing or two about Welsh poetry and drama. According to the newsletter of the Chelmsford and District Welsh Society, the Phoenix Players 'come with a wonderful reputation for this fascinating play'.

MAY 1ST

1997: Bob Russell, a Liberal Democrat, became Colchester's MP on this day. The one thing that can be said of Bob Russell is that he is definitely a local man; which is perhaps a good deal of his appeal. Before becoming an MP, he was a local councillor for twenty years; being at different times Mayor of Colchester and leader of the council. On the minus side, Sir Bob, as he has been since the 2012 New Years' Honours List, seems to have astonishingly flexible political beliefs. His ideology has allowed him at different times to accommodate himself to three different political parties; Labour, Social Democrats and Liberals.

Colchester had a very strong tradition of being Conservative and it took a remarkable man to reverse that trend not just once, but at four General Elections in 1997, 2001, 2005 and 2010. Strange to think that had circumstances been a little different, Sir Bob might now be sitting on the opposition benches. In 1979, he stood for Parliament as a Labour candidate. As things are now, he has become a much-loved figure in the town and it would be a rash man who could foresee his losing an election in the future; for whichever party he chooses to stand.

MAY 2ND

2011: Red Kites were spotted flying above Colchester Zoo on this day. Zoo staff were so excited about this that on May 20th they issued a press release on the subject. It seems that the first Red Kite, a male, was spotted on May 2nd, flying above the falconry display which featured a Black Kite. Since then, the bird was seen at least three times a week. On May 4th, a female Red Kite was also seen.

Red Kites were driven almost to extinction in the nineteenth century and by the mid-1980s existed only in a small stronghold in the mountains about Aberystwyth in Wales. An attempt was made a few years later to reintroduce them to England; specifically along the line of the A40 between London and Oxford. This experiment was a brilliant success; the great birds of prey being as commonly seen in the area as starlings. There have been signs in recent years that the Red Kites are colonising other parts of the country, but the ones seen near Colchester Zoo are the first to be seen in this part of Essex. The zoo attributed the appearance of these unusual birds to a new nature area which they had laid out, which has attracted buzzards and kestrels. The hope is that the Kites will now stay in the area and begin to breed.

MAY 3RD

2010: The *Daily Gazette* reported on this day that there was considerable opposition to the expansion of Colchester's only mosque. Unease about the mosque seemed to be motivated less by Islamophobia than by quite understandable concerns about noise and disruption. The mosque, which occupies numbers 2-3 Priory Street, had originally been set up without any sort of planning permission. The two small houses had had internal walls knocked down to make a space for prayer and the council had in effect been presented with a *fait accompli*.

At a meeting of the Planning Committee, the mosque requested retroactive planning permission, after having concreted over the gardens of the two houses to make parking spaces. Neighbours claimed that up to 250 worshippers now used the place, which was in a residential area. It was stated that outdoor prayers were being held and that large numbers of children were making a noise.

The council granted two years permission for the creation by the mosque of hard standing, but suggested that they might think about new and larger premises as it appeared to the members of the committee that perhaps they had outgrown the present site.

MAY 4TH

1847: On this day Isaac Pooley, a shoemaker living in Colchester, wrote his will. It was rare in the mid-nineteenth century for an artisan of this sort to prepare a will, but then Isaac Pooley was no ordinary shoemaker.

In 1805, a sea battle took place which would decide the future of Europe. Would the French dictator Napoleon Bonaparte control the sea lanes? Every schoolboy knows that the British Admiral Nelson triumphed at this most famous of naval engagements, which took place off an obscure cape in southern Spain called Trafalgar.

One of those who manned the guns on Nelson's flagship, HMS *Victory*, was a Colchester man, none other than Isaac Pooley. After the end of the Napoleonic wars he settled down at Hythe Hill and worked quietly as a cobbler for the next sixty years or so, until his death in 1871.

In 2006, Isaac Pooley's grave was rediscovered in Colchester Cemetery on Mersea Road. It has now been cleaned and is being well maintained again, as befits the last resting place of somebody who played such a crucial, if humble, role in the history of Europe.

MAY 5TH

1848: On this day, William Wire recorded in his diary what was being uncovered during the building of the hospital which was to be attached to Colchester's workhouse:

> I visited the excavations for the foundations of the infirmary at the Union House. Only a few fragments of pottery have been discovered, but a foundation at the NW corner running west, made with fragments of Roman roof tiles and bricks, cemented together with a loose kind of mortar.

The hospital, together with the existing workhouse buildings, later became St Mary's Hospital. This has now been demolished and replaced by a multi-storey car park.

What Wire did not know was that this site, which lays outside the Roman city walls near the Balkerne Gate, was in fact an early example of a suburb. Roman Colchester had been sprawling across a pretty large area, with no defensive walls at all when Boudicca and her army attacked it in AD 60. After the recovery of the town, the decision was made to erect walls. The area around the old St Mary's Hospital was left outside the walls. Perhaps this explains why the archaeological evidence suggests that this little suburb was at its height in the late first century AD, but seemed to decline after that period. This would have coincided with the building of the city walls.

MAY 6TH

2011: On this day, a typography exhibition began at The Gallery in Colchester. Colchester has quite a few galleries, theatres and museums; ranging from the large and imposing to the small and all but unknown. It is to this latter category that The Gallery belongs. It is the newest of the town's cultural spaces, having only opened on November 24th 2010. The small gallery is the brainchild of graphic artist Lee Thomas. The intention is to focus exclusively upon contemporary art, graphic design, photography and illustration. The Gallery opens from 9 a.m. to 5 p.m. on Thursdays, Fridays and Saturdays and revolves around specific displays which change from time to time. The typography exhibition is typical of the sort of quirky but intriguing subjects chosen for the place.

Lee Thomas said that he has always loved small, contemporary galleries and that he had been trying for some time to find a suitable location where he would be able to showcase his own work and that of other artists and designers whom he admired. The Gallery, at 20 Church Walk, will be developing over the coming years.

May 7th

1971: This is the day that the first ever Gay Lib meeting was held in Colchester – at the University of Essex campus. The Gay Liberation Front had strong support in the university, which was well known for the generally left-wing attitude of both students and lecturers. The local press did not seem unsympathetic to Gay Lib: when the student magazine at the university published an article headed 'Gay is Good', the *Colchester Evening Gazette* commented upon it.

By 1974, the Gay Libbers on the Essex campus had become a little more assertive. An article appeared in the student magazine on November 11th, asking all students to be aware of the struggle which gay people faced. The following year, a Gay Week was held at the university; an event which the *Colchester Evening Gazette* was happy to advertise. In 1976, the Essex Gay Liberation Front changed their name to the Gay Society. Perhaps by this time they felt that their struggle for recognition had been successful and that it was as acceptable to be gay as it was to be heterosexual.

MAY 8TH

1936: The 5th Colchester Scout group, which was based at St Botolph's Church, was registered by John Arnott on this day. It was originally a detachment of the 33rd Colchester Scouts. In 1982, the two groups merged together and have been known as the 5th Colchester Scouts ever since. In 1965, a wooden hut was built in Queen Elizabeth Way which housed the 33rd Colchester troop and later the combined 5th and 33rd groups. This was demolished in 2007 and replaced with a brick building – paid for by a grant from Colchester Borough Council.

Scouting used to be a tremendously popular hobby for boys of secondary school age. A survey in the 1970s revealed that a third of all adults had belonged to either the Boy Scouts or Girl Guides when younger. Sadly, with so many other exciting things to do, Scouting has declined somewhat in popularity for teenage boys. Although the 5th Colchester currently has Beavers and Cub Scouts, they do not have a Scout section, although it is hoped that this can be re-launched in the future.

MAY 9TH

2010: The Colchester and District Pipes and Drums band played in Holland on this day. Started in January 2010, the band claims to be the fasted growing and most dynamic pipe band in the United Kingdom. Quite how one measures the dynamism of a pipe band has not been explained.

The Colchester and District Pipes and Drums have their own tartan called, unsurprisingly, the Colchester and District Tartan. The colours are based upon Colchester's coat of arms. They are available for carnivals, fêtes, corporate entertainment, weddings and 'birthday surprises'.

Among the testimonials on their website are one from the Tendring Hall Open Garden. Since the message is signed by somebody called Alistair and ends with 'Yours aye', it is probably reasonable to assume that he is genuinely Scottish and therefore knows a bit about bagpipes. He attributes almost superhuman powers to the Colchester and District Pipes and Drums, saying, 'I write to say what a stunning performance was given by your pipes and drums band on Sunday. The setting was marvellous and the sun shone'.

MAY 10TH

1972: Colchester's Mercury Theatre opened on this day. In 1937, the Colchester Repertory Company was formed. They performed in various locations, but always had as their ultimate goal a theatre of their own. They mainly played in a makeshift theatre in the High Road, which had been converted from the old assembly rooms and former art gallery. After some great feats of fundraising, the money for this project was acquired in the late 1960s and architect Norman Downie was commissioned to design a thoroughly modern theatre for the company. The Mercury Theatre also contains the Digby Gallery, where local artists display their work.

In construction, the Mercury is almost identical to the Salisbury Playhouse. This is hardly surprising, since they were both designed by the same person. The stage is hexagonal, but can be converted to a proscenium arch style by moveable pillars. In addition to the main theatre, there is a smaller studio theatre: with only seventy-five seats, this has a more intimate feel.

MAY 11TH

1836: The foundation stone of St Botolph's Church was laid on this day by John Round. The parish had been without a church for almost 200 years.

We are so used to nineteenth-century churches being in Gothic Revival style, that it comes as a surprise to come across a church like this, which was built only a couple of years before Victoria's accession to the throne and shows no trace at all of Gothic architecture. The architect turned instead to the neighbouring ruins of St Botolph's Priory for inspiration; the overall style being Romanesque, with the arches being round rather than pointed. It is uncommon to find this effect in a brick-built church and it would be easy to dismiss it as mere pastiche, except that the false columns and arcades on the tower of St Botolph's Church reflect the priory in a way that suggests a tribute rather than a vulgar copy. The fact that the priory itself was built largely of Roman bricks helps matters.

It is hard to believe that a high Victorian, neo-Gothic edifice would have fitted into the space as sympathetically as the present building does.

MAY 12TH

2011: The BBC programme *Antiques Roadshow* was filmed at Layer Marney on this day. Layer Marney is famous for one thing; the enormous Tudor gatehouse which is the tallest in the country. The 80-foot structure, built of a rare combination of terracotta and brick, looks like a palace in itself. It is extraordinary to think that this ambitious and imposing building was in fact no more than the entrance to the grounds containing the main house. In the event, the house was never to be built. With the death of Lord Marney in 1523, followed only two years later by that of his son, the family ran out of male heirs and the estate was broken up. The mighty gatehouse alone remains, towering above the surrounding countryside like some bizarre folly.

A lot of damage was caused to the Layer Marney gateway and the other surviving buildings in the grounds by the 1884 earthquake. According to *The Builder* magazine, a few years later the tower was practically a crumbling ruin and the amount of money needed to repair it was likely to be 'so large that the chance of the work ever being done appears remote indeed'. Fortunately, a brother and sister called Peache re-roofed the tower and from then it passed to several other owners who were prepared to invest in the fabric of this remarkable building. Since 1959 it has been owned by the Charrington family. Layer Marney Tower can be visited in the summer and also hired out for weddings and other events.

MAY 13TH

1845: On this day, the *David Malcolm*, loaded with prisoners bound for transportation, set sail for Van Dieman's Land and Norfolk Island. The practice of transporting convicted felons to the colonies began when America was still a British possession. When we lost the American War of Independence, Australia became a good alternative. Some criminals were transported for life, although the great majority were only exiled for a set number of years. The catch was that after their sentence had expired, most did not have the funds to purchase a ticket back to this country and so were forced to remain in Australia.

Some of the offences for which people were transported were, by today's standards, unbelievably trivial. One of those transported to Van Dieman's Land on the *David Malcolm* was James Chaplin from Essex. His neighbour dealt in pigs and had bought eighty-seven at market in Colchester. One went missing and tracks led to James Chaplin's rabbit pen. His rather unconvincing explanation was that the pig must have wandered there of its own accord. This cut no ice with the court, where Chaplin received the sentence of seven years' transportation. There is no record of his ever returning home.

MAY 14TH

1943: This day was the last dress rehearsal and final practice for the Dambuster raids, which were to take place two days later. In his autobiography, Guy Gibson, leader of the raid by 617 Squadron, refers to 'the Colchester lake'. In fact the training took place at Abberton Reservoir, a few miles from Colchester. This was roughly the same size and shape as the reservoir behind the Eder Dam in Germany, which was attacked after the Mohne Dam.

The Layer Causeway at Abberton was used as the target for practice runs with the bouncing bombs which would be used for the raids on the Ruhr dams. The flat Essex countryside was perfect for the Lancaster bombers to refine the tricky, low level approaches, which would be necessary for the attacks on the German dams. Time and again, the bombers of 617 Squadron flew in over Abberton and released the bouncing bombs. The attack itself was scheduled to take place on May 16th 1943 and so the final rehearsal was of crucial importance. It went smoothly and during the actual raid, the dams were breached in textbook style. Abberton had played a vital role in one of the most famous missions of the Second World War.

MAY 15TH

1902: Colchester's new Town Hall opened on this day. The site of the Town Hall has been the focus of civic life in the town since 1160, for it is where the old Moot Hall once stood. Construction of the present Town Hall was begun in 1898. The previous year, a competition had been held to see who would have the task of designing the building. This was won by John Belcher. The Earl of Rosebery, Prime Minister at the time, performed the opening ceremony.

Colchester Town Hall is built in the Baroque style so beloved of the Victorians. It is surmounted by 162-foot high tower, bearing a statue not of St Helena, the patron saint of Colchester, as some suppose, but the Virgin Mary. Perhaps the most impressive part of the building is the Council Chamber. This has an elaborately painted ceiling showing the twelve months of the year in Classical form. The room is also lit by two huge stained-glass windows which depict the Roman history of Colchester and the surrounding district. So beautifully decorated is this room that the council now rent it out as a venue for weddings and civil partnerships.

In 2011, plans were made to privatise the Town Hall by hiring a company to market and run the building. It was felt that a private company might be able to recoup some of the money that was being lost each year while it was being run by the local authority.

MAY 16TH

1947: The *London Gazette* announced on this day that Field Marshal Wavell, perhaps the greatest British soldier of the Second World War, was to be made an Earl. This honour was eclipsed later that same year, when he was appointed High Steward of Colchester. The report in the *London Gazette* says:

> The King has been pleased under Letters Patent under the Great Seal of the Realm, bearing date the 1st instant, to confer the dignity of a Viscount and Earl of the United Kingdom upon Field Marshal the Right Honourable Archibald Percival, Viscount Wavell, G.C.B., G.C.S.I., C.M.G., M.C., and the heirs male of his body lawfully begotten, by the Name, style and title Viscount Kerren, of Eritrea and of Winchester in the County of Southampton and EARL WAVELL.

Although it is a purely ceremonial post, conferring no advantage, it is an ancient position and all those who have held it seem to have been keenly aware that it is not bestowed lightly. Viscount Wavell remained High Steward of Colchester until his death in 1950. Along the way, he collected other honours, including Constable of the Tower in 1948 and Lord-Lieutenant of London in 1949.

MAY 17TH

1778: Marianne Nunn was born in Colchester on this day. She did not marry and lived a quiet, one might almost say secretive, life. She is chiefly remembered today for the hymns she wrote; one in particular still being very popular. *One There is Above All Others* is only a short hymn, but it has had a great deal of influence, being particularly popular in America. Miss Nunn's brother, who was a minister, published it first in a book called *Psalms and Hymns*:

> One there is above all others,
> Oh, how He loves,
> His is love beyond a brother's
> Oh, how He loves,
> Earthly friends may fail or leave us,
> One day soothe; the next day grieve us,
> But this friend will ne'er deceive us,
> Oh, how He loves.

This style of sacred poetry is, from a technical point, very well constructed. There are another three verses and a notable point is the number of Biblical references which are worked into the hymn. Marianne Nunn died in Colchester on February 27th 1847.

MAY 18TH

2011: The first Mayor of Colchester to have been born abroad was installed on this day. Of Chinese ancestry, Helen Chuah moved to Colchester in 1971, having previously been living on the island of Penang in the Far East. The Councillor for St Anne's ward was filmed by television crews from Malaysia and China as she took the oath, donned the ceremonial robes and received the Chain of Office at Colchester's Moot Hall.

Present at the Mayor-making ceremony was Ms Chuah's partner; Councillor Mike Hogg. He had himself been Mayor a decade earlier. Helen Chuah came to this country from Georgetown in Penang, which is part of Malaysia, in order to train as a nurse. After she qualified, she raised her family while also working full-time. She was first elected as a councillor in 1988 and a few years later joined the Colchester Centurion Rotarian Club, with the object of promoting world peace and international understanding.

The decision to make Helen Chua the Mayor of Colchester attracted favourable attention to the town across the world, and particularly in the Far East, where it was seen to symbolise the possibilities for advancement for Chinese people living in Europe.

MAY 19TH

1614: This is the day that John Bastwick, who was born at Writtle in Essex, entered Cambridge University. He spent only a short time at Emmanuel College before falling out with his tutors and leaving. He then went abroad and studied in Italy to become a doctor. After qualifying, he returned to England and settled in Colchester. At this point, John Bastwick's life seemed fairly straightforward and settled. He built up a good practice as a physician in Colchester and could have lived there happily with no further trouble.

Unfortunately, Bastwick had very strong religious opinions, which brought him into conflict with the Archbishop of Canterbury when he published them in the form of a book; *Elunchus Religionis Papistcae*. Although written in Latin and published in the Netherlands, this attack on the established Church was enough to have him arrested and imprisoned. While in prison, he wrote another book, this time in English, in which he denounced bishops as the enemies of God. For this, he was tried again and sentenced to stand in the pillory, have his ears cut off, pay a fine of £5,000 and be imprisoned for life. By all accounts, he endured the savage punishment bravely and was later released during the English Civil War.

MAY 20TH

1904: Margery Allingham, the thriller writer, was born on this day. Although she became famous for her crime stories, featuring the detective Albert Campion, her first novel was something entirely different.

In 1921, 17-year-old Margery went with her family on holiday to Mersea Island. While there, a number of light-hearted séances were held, which supposedly resulted in contact with the spirit of a smuggler. This led Margery to write a book based upon smugglers operating on Mersea Island during the eighteenth century: *Blackkerchief Dick* was published in 1923. Although it received good reviews, Margery was embarrassed by the book and did not want it to be reprinted when she later became famous for her contemporary thrillers.

Something about Mersea seemed to stimulate Margery's creativity, because *Blackkerchief Dick* was not the only novel which she wrote set there. *Mystery Mile,* an Albert Campion book, was apparently set in Sussex, but the descriptions of the landscape are quite plainly Mersea Island. The climax of the novel takes place in salt marshes identical to those which surround Mersea.

MAY 21ST

1956: Harry Bensley, one of the last great British eccentrics, died on this day. Born in the Norfolk town of Thetford in 1876, Bensley was a notorious gambler. As a result of a wager – the precise circumstances of which are obscure – he agreed to travel first around 169 British cities and towns, before travelling to another eighteen foreign countries. He was to do this while pushing a pram and wearing an iron helmet from a suit of armour. The only way that he was allowed to support himself was by selling postcards. In addition to this, he had to get married without revealing his face to his future wife!

Bensley set off from Trafalgar Square on January 1st 1908 and spent the next six years on the road. The outbreak of the First World War found him in Italy and he returned home and enlisted in the army. After the war was over, Bensley, now penniless, settled in Wivenhoe. He had a succession of fairly low paid jobs such as doorman at a cinema and warden at a YMCA hostel. He was also twice elected as a Labour councillor.

As the years passed, Harry Bensley became more and more impoverished. No longer was he the daring young man who had once tried to walk round the world for a bet. During the Second World War, he worked in an ammunition factory, dying alone in a bedsit at the age of 80.

MAY 22ND

1928: Colchester's first motor buses began running on this day. For the last twenty-five years or so, Colchester Corporation had been running trams, but after a couple of decades, a problem arose. The day-to-day running of the electric trams had been budgeted for over the years, but not the astronomical cost of replacing the infrastructure of the system when it eventually wore out. The rails and wires would all need to be replaced and when this cost was examined, it was thought to be more economically sound to scrap the trams entirely and use buses instead.

From the beginning, Colchester Council were determined that they would run the buses themselves and not pay any external company to do so on their behalf. A number of companies, such as the National Omnibus Company, approached the council and offered a competitive service, but they were all refused. The first buses were single-deckers, but in 1929 double-deckers were introduced. The last trams in Colchester made their journeys on December 9th 1929.

Colchester Council continued to insist on operating their own transport right up until the reforms of the Thatcher years, when practically everything in sight was being privatised.

MAY 23RD

2005: On this day, The Badger Trust was incorporated as a company. The North East Essex branch of the Badger Trust is based in Colchester. They are one of eighty such groups throughout the country. Their website boasts that they have a 'badger hotline' which is manned twenty-four hours a day to deal with all matters relating to badgers in North East Essex. It is apparently 'important that any dead badger found on the road is dealt with quickly and removed from the location'. Other duties of those operating the 'badger hotline' include advising people what to do if they have unwanted badgers in their garden.

MAY 24TH

1995: This is the day that the Triratna Buddhist Community was registered as a charity with the Charity Commission. In 1998, this group opened the Colchester Buddhist Centre at 11 Manor Road. The centre offers classes in meditation and information about Buddhism.

The Triratna (from the Sanskrit for 'three jewels') Buddhist Order was formerly known as the Friends of the Western Buddhist Order and was founded in this country in 1967. Essentially, it is the Buddhist equivalent of an ecumenical group which hopes to synthesise Buddhism with various Western traditions. The Friends of the Western Buddhist Order was started by a Buddhist monk known by some as Sangharakshita and by others as Dennis Lingwood, from South London.

MAY 25TH

1868: Sabine Baring-Gould was married on this day. After attending Cambridge, he took holy orders and in 1871 was appointed the rector of the village of East Mersea. This is the smaller of the two settlements on Mersea Island. The sheer scale and variety of Baring-Gould's achievements makes one almost giddy. He wrote several of our most popular hymns, including *Onwards Christian Soldiers* and *Now the Day is Over*. He was also the author of the standard reference work on lycanthropy. *The Book of Were-Wolves*, published in 1865, is still the most cited book on this topic. Among his other works were a sixteen-volume history of the lives of the saints, an erudite work on medieval mythology, and various biographies and travel books.

Sabine Baring-Gould also wrote many novels. One of these, *Mehalah; a story of the Salt Marshes*, was described by one critic as 'the Wuthering Heights of Essex'. Set during the Napoleonic Wars, the action of the novel takes place almost exclusively on Mersea and the nearby Ray island.

MAY 26TH

2011: Colchester Council's Planning Committee met on this day to discuss the controversial Horkesley Park development. This development was intended to be a 'heritage centre' in North Essex, next to Dedham Vale and right in the middle of some of the loveliest countryside in East Anglia. It would consist of a 100-acre country park, an art gallery and a craft studio. The only slight problem is that nobody except for the company promoting the development seemed to want the thing.

Bunting & Sons, the company so eager to transform a large stretch of countryside into a heritage centre, claim that it would attract almost half a million visitors each year and create many new jobs in the area. The Stour Valley Action Group, who coordinated opposition to the scheme, have fought long and hard to have it abandoned entirely. They make the very good point that the proposed heritage park would charge visitors £10 for visiting exactly the same countryside which is at the moment available to enjoy for free. In the end, Colchester Council rejected the idea and Bunting & Sons, who have bought a lot of land near Dedham, are, at the time of writing, planning a new application.

MAY 27TH

2011: This day marked the deadline for Colchester once again to apply for city status. Becoming a city in Britain is not just a question of having a certain number of people living in one place or occupying a large enough area. The designation of city status is the gift of the monarch and she alone can decide whether or not a town has the right to call itself a city. Nor can one apply for this status at any time; there are special years when competitions are held for those towns which think that they deserve to be promoted to cities.

Colchester has applied for city status twice in the past. Once was in 2000, to mark the new millennium, and the second occasion was during the Queen's Golden Jubilee in 2002.

There are arguments both for and against the idea of Colchester becoming a city. Currently, there is not the least dispute that Colchester is the oldest town in Britain. Would it be advantageous to exchange this for the designation of being instead the newest city? On the other hand, it has the first castle to be a Royal castle outside London, the oldest city walls in Britain, and has recently applied for World Heritage Site status. The debate continues, but the application was duly submitted by the council before the closing date, and failed. Chelmsford, the county town of Essex, won the award instead.

MAY 28TH

2011: A pilgrimage to Walsingham left East Hill in Colchester at 8 a.m., bound for the shrine in Norfolk. It was organised by the Catholic church of St James the Less and St Helen.

Today, the shrine of Our lady at Walsingham is an exceedingly East Anglian place of pilgrimage, but for several centuries it was one of northern Europe's most popular sites of pilgrimage. In the early eleventh century, a Saxon noblewoman had a dream about Walsingham, which consists of two small villages; Little Walsingham and Great Walsingham. Richeldis de Faverches felt that she was under a religious duty to build a replica of Christ's family home in Nazareth. She did so and Walsingham became the pilgrimage of choice for those who were unable or unwilling to go trekking all the way to the Holy Land to visit the real Nazareth.

Walsingham was suppressed during the Reformation, but its fortunes revived in the twentieth century. There are both Catholic and Anglican shrines now at Walsingham and adherents to both branches of Christianity make the pilgrimage there, usually by coach.

MAY 29TH

1645: On this day, Mary Cook died in Colchester Castle at 3 o'clock in the afternoon. According to the subsequent inquest, she died by 'divine intervention', which is the archaic way of describing what we today would call 'natural causes'. Mary was one of a number of women being held in the castle as a result of Matthew Hopkins – the self-styled 'Witchfinder General'. Such were the conditions in the cells that death was by no means uncommon among prisoners. On May 7th in the same year, for example, Joan Cooper also died from 'natural causes', while on June 11th, Rose Hallybread was recorded as having died from 'divine visitation'. The cramped and unsanitary conditions in the prison were such as to promote the spread of infectious diseases, which were usually called by the generic term, 'gaol fever'.

MAY 30TH

1858: On this day, the Methodists at Lexden held a camp meeting, changing the location from Kelvedon, where it was originally to be held. They later held camp meetings at many other locations around Colchester.

The camp meeting was an essentially Methodist phenomenon, although not all Methodists approved of them. In a camp meeting, people travel from all over a wide area and pitch tents at some field. Preachers then organise meetings, Bible study classes and sessions of prayer. Outsiders were welcomed to these events and such was the atmosphere generated, that many of those who came as casual visitors were converted to Christianity. The Wesleyan Methodists did not really hold with such goings-on and so those who were enthusiastic advocates of camp meetings split off and formed the Primitive Methodists. It was to this strand of Methodism that the group in Lexden belonged. Throughout the 1850s and '60s, such meetings were held at Brightlingsea, Fingringhoe, Wivenhoe and many other places near Colchester.

MAY 31ST

2011: The *Daily Gazette* reported on this day that 600 members of 16 Air Assault Brigade were to march through Colchester on June 7th as part of a homecoming parade. The troops had been fighting in Afghanistan and were being given the Freedom of the Borough of Colchester. The intention was that the soldiers would march, 'with swords drawn, bayonets fixed, drums beating, bands playing and colours flying'.

As a garrison town, Colchester has witnessed military displays of this sort many times before. When the parade took place, thousands of Colchester's residents turned out to line the streets. The soldiers were cheered as they passed, being led by the Band of the Parachute regiment. The salute was taken at the Town Hall by Helen Chuah, Mayor of Colchester; Lord Petre, the Lord-Lieutenant of Essex and Brigadier James Chiswell, who commanded the brigade in Afghanistan. The following day, members of the brigade attended a welcome home service at Bury St Edmunds Cathedral in Suffolk.

JUNE 1ST

1977: John Morris, author of *The Age of Arthur*, died on this day. *The Age of Arthur*, published in 1973 when Morris was 60, was an attempt to investigate the Dark Age which engulfed Britain after the Romans left. Morris studied history at Cambridge and was for a time lecturer in Ancient History at University College London. Despite this, *The Age of Arthur* was not well received and was widely supposed to have caused irreparable damage to his reputation as a serious historian.

Colchester was central to Morris' theme, as developed in *The Age of Arthur*. He claimed that the Romanised Britons who lived in this country during the Dark Age looked back to a mythical golden age of peace, civilisation and order. What could be more natural for them than to associate this with the former capital of Britain, Camulodunum, which later became known as Colchester. According to Morris, the name Camulodunum became corrupted over the years and shortened to Camelot. It is an intriguing idea, for which there is, unfortunately, not a shred of evidence. Morris is the only mainstream historian ever to suggest that Camelot was in Essex; many others favouring Cadbury Castle in Somerset.

JUNE 2ND

1975: This is the day that snow stopped play during the Essex *v.* Kent cricket match being held in Castle Park in Colchester. Since cricket is a summer game, its being interrupted by snow in this country is, to say the least, rare. Overall, the summer of 1975 was one of the warmest on record. On Saturday, May 31st that year, Colchester was enjoying a particularly pleasant spell of sunny weather. County championship cricket matches were being played across the whole country and Colchester was the scene of some spirited games between Essex and Kent.

On the Monday morning, a bitterly cold wind blew down from the north, bringing with it rain and then sleet; followed, almost unbelievably, by snow. In Buxton, the highest town in England, play between Derbyshire and Lancashire was abandoned as snow covered the pitch. In Colchester, the players managed to struggle on for two hours through some bitterly cold conditions, but when the sleet turned to snow, the match was halted.

Snow even fell as far south as London; John Arlott reporting in the *Guardian* that it snowed during a cricket match at Lords.

JUNE 3RD

1817: Charles Abbot, born in Colchester and Speaker of the House, was made Baron Colchester on this day. Born in 1757, his father was the Rector of All Saints in Colchester. His half-brother was Jeremy Bentham, the famous Utilitarian philosopher.

Abbot's first career was in the law and he qualified and practiced as a barrister for twelve years before entering Parliament in 1795 as the MP for Helston. He became very involved with various committees in Parliament and was instrumental in pushing for a nationwide census; which had never before been undertaken in this country. The first census, which was held in 1801, was largely a product of Charles Abbot's efforts.

In 1802, Abbot was made Speaker of the House of Commons, a position which he held for the next fifteen years. By the time he was sixty he was suffering badly from the skin disease Erysipelas, and this eventually compelled him to retire from politics for good in 1817. He was made Baron Colchester and spent the last twelve years of his life in happy retirement, dying in 1829 and passing the title of Baron Colchester to his eldest son.

JUNE 4TH

2011: On this day, the tradition of Archer of the Fayre was revived in Colchester. The event was organised by the Colchester Town Watch, an historical re-enactment society, and all the participants dressed in period costume and used proper longbows for the contest. The event was won by Mick Baily.

Events included speed shooting, where the object was to loose off as many arrows as possible over a period of thirty seconds, with additional points for arrows which actually hit the target, and wolf and boar shoots, all at inanimate targets. For those hoping to compete in future years, the conditions are fairly strict. All entrants must be members of archery clubs, well versed in the use of the English longbow, and also belong to a medieval re-enactment society which holds archery contests as a major part of its activities. All those entering must wear appropriate costume from the fourteenth to sixteenth centuries, although glasses are allowed to be worn. These stringent rules are necessary in order for the organisers to obtain Public Liability Insurance against the possibility of any spectators being injured by inexperienced bowmen.

JUNE 5TH

1884: The edition of the British scientific magazine *Nature*, which was published on this day, had a full and detailed account of the earthquake which struck Colchester on April 22nd that year. The article ran through tremors and earthquakes which had struck Britain over the last few centuries and concluded that this was the worst earthquake since the one which struck the Dover Straits in 1580. It was noted that although there was considerable damage, this was patchy, with some parts of Essex being more greatly affected than others. In the village of Peldon, for example, every single building was damaged to a greater or lesser extent, while a few miles away there was hardly any structural damage at all.

One of the most vexed questions following the Colchester earthquake was the death toll; if, that is, anybody had been killed by it at all. *The Times* reported that a child in the village of Rowhedge had been killed, but did not supply a name. Other reports placed the number who died at three, four or five. It is entirely possible that one or two people were struck by falling masonry from chimneys and so on, but without a name and death certificate to examine, such claims are open to doubt.

JUNE 6TH

1944: This was D-Day; the day that allied forces began the invasion of Europe and its liberation from occupation by the Nazis. The town of Wivenhoe, a few miles from Colchester, played a small role on this momentous occasion.

Following the disastrous Dieppe Raid in 1942, it was obvious that any invading allied force could not rely upon landing men and supplies at harbours captured from the Germans. The decision was accordingly made to construct harbours in this country in pre-fabricated sections and then tow them across the Channel for the D-Day landings. The logistics of the operation were staggering and the building and transport of these temporary harbours is often cited as a model of military engineering.

The codename for the harbours used during the Normandy landings was 'Mulberry' and they required various components: floating roadways, breakwaters and piers. On the Old Ferry Marsh at Wivenhoe, two enormous steel pier heads, codenamed 'whales', were constructed. These were 200 feet long and 60 feet wide. They each stood on four legs which could be raised or lowered to compensate for tides.

JUNE 7TH

1662: Celia Fiennes was born in Wiltshire on this day. Following a bout of illness, Celia decided at the age of 22 to travel around England, 'to regain my health by variety and a change of air and exercise'. Travelling simply for the sake of it at that time was an unheard of thing, and particularly odd for a woman to undertake such a journey. The result was a perfect description of the country towards the end of the seventeenth century. *Through England on a Side Saddle* became a Restoration bestseller and is still in print to this day. Fiennes visited was Colchester and she gives a succinct description of the town in 1685:

> Colchester is a large town. You enter the town by a gate. There are four in all. There is a large street which runs a great length down to the bridge, it's nearly a mile long. Through the middle of it runs another broad street nearly the same length in which is the Market Cross and Town Hall and a long building, like stalls, on which they lay their bays, exposed for sale. Great quantities are made here and sent in bales to London. The whole town is employed in spinning, weaving, washing, drying and dressing their bays in which they seem very industrious.

Celia Fiennes is widely recognised as the first woman known to have visited every county in England.

JUNE 8TH

1949: It is a matter of some regret to those living in Colchester that their home town does not appear in many books or films. Some parts of the country, Notting Hill for example, always seem to be cropping up in fiction. Colchester is, by comparison, all but unknown. There is one striking exception; a world-famous book which makes explicit mention of the town, albeit in a rather unfortunate context.

On June 8th 1949, George Orwell's dystopian vision of a future Britain ruled as a totalitarian dictatorship was published. In *Nineteen Eighty-Four*, an extended world war has demolished the world's existing blocs and divided the planet into three vast empires; Eurasia, Eastasia and Oceania. Britain has been renamed Airstrip One and is in essence no more than a military base off the coast of Europe. Remembering the wars which led to this situation during his childhood, the book's protagonist, Winston Smith, muses, 'Perhaps it was the time when the atomic bomb had fallen on Colchester.' That is pretty much it for literary references to the town, apart from the first part of *Moll Flanders* by Daniel Defoe, which is largely set in Colchester.

JUNE 9TH

2011: The *Daily Gazette* reported on this day that Colchester and Ipswich Museum Service had submitted a £4.2 million bid to the National Lottery, in an attempt to secure sufficient funds to renovate and update completely the interior of Colchester's Norman Castle. The castle contains Colchester Museum and it is some while since there has been a wholesale redevelopment. The castle is a thousand years old and it stands upon the foundations of a 2,000-year-old Roman temple, but none of this is immediately apparent to those visiting the museum. A survey of visitors found that many wished to feel that they were in a castle when they went to the museum. As things are currently arranged, the whole of the interior is packed with information plaques, cases and wooden walkways. One has no sense at all of being within a remarkable historic building.

In recent years, a number of dramatic finds from the Roman and pre-Roman eras have been unearthed and the Museum Service wish to be able to display these. Such finds include a 1,200 coin hoard from the site of the old barracks, and remains from the recently discovered chariot track.

June 10th

1530: John Beche, also known as Thomas Marshall, was appointed Abbot of St John's Abbey in Colchester on this day. Four years later, he took the Oath of Supremacy, acknowledging Henry VIII to be the head of the Church in this country, rather than the Pope. The following year though, things started to go wrong for the Abbot. King Henry was busily dismantling the convents and monasteries of England and executing any of the monks who opposed him in this enterprise. John Beche was heard expressing sympathy with some of those who had been executed for their supposed treason over this business.

Beche was arrested in 1538 and sent to the Tower of London, accused of high treason. Witnesses claimed that the Abbot had been heard to say that Thomas More and others had, 'died like good men and it was pity of their deaths'. Even worse, he had stated that the dissolution of the monasteries and the break with Rome had come about because of the king's desire to marry Anne Boleyn. All true enough of course, but exceedingly tactless and dangerous views to be heard uttering at the height of the Reformation.

The former Abbot was taken back to Colchester and on December 1st 1539, he was hanged over the gateway of his own abbey, cut down while still alive and then castrated and disembowelled.

On May 13th 1895, Pope Leo XIII announced John Beche's beatification and he is known to Catholics today as the Blessed John Beche.

JUNE 11TH

1834: The windmill at Old Heath Road Mill was blown down in a storm on this day. At one time, Colchester had thirty or so windmills dotted around the town and surrounding countryside. Before the Industrial Revolution and the introduction of steam power, wind provided the most effective source of power for milling grain into flour.

Just as in our own time we have seen wind turbines unable to cope with high winds, so too was this a problem for windmills in the eighteenth and nineteenth centuries. Quite a few near Colchester either blew down or caught fire. The Old Heath Road Mill was not the only one to be demolished by gales. The year before, the Dunnages Mill had suffered the same fate – in June 1833 – barely six months after it had been built. In 1836, Clubbs Mill was blown down in high winds. A replacement was built in 1838, but this too succumbed to the wind in 1852.

The windmills which did not blow down often seemed to have gone up in flames. Butt Mill burned down in 1787, just five years after it had been built. The same thing happened to St Ann's Mill. In 1807, Mile End Mill also burned down. Some windmills lasted only a matter of months. An experimental horizontal windmill was erected on top of Colchester Castle in 1834 but removed the same year, as it was found to be inefficient compared with more conventional windmills.

JUNE 12TH

2010: On this day, an episode of *Dr Who* called 'The Lodger' was broadcast. It was certainly the first episode of *Dr Who* to be set entirely in Colchester and possibly the first episode of any British television serial to be shot entirely in the town. Whether this was connected with the location or not, it is impossible to say, but this episode had fewer viewers than any other in that particular series of *Dr Who*; it was watched by just 6.44 million viewers. Curiously enough, it also received the highest appreciation index of the series from those who did watch it.

After the TARDIS lands in modern-day Colchester, it dematerializes, leaving the Doctor stranded. He rents a bedsit in an apparently ordinary house in Colchester. In fact, part of the house turns out to be a disguised alien spaceship, which is luring passers-by in; whereupon they promptly vanish. The owner of the house is an unexceptional resident of Colchester, who is secretly in love with a young woman with whom he works. The spaceship is really trying desperately to acquire a new pilot, which accounts for the passers-by who were lured into the ship, which has disguised itself as the second floor of the house.

The resolution sees the owner of the house united with the object of his love and the Doctor reunited with the TARDIS.

June 13th

1648: This day marks the beginning of the Siege of Colchester in the English Civil War. Royalist forces led by the Earl of Norwich established themselves in the town and after a brief battle, the Parliamentary forces decided that they could not dislodge the Royalists from the town by force and so surrounded the walls and tried to starve them into surrender.

By July 2nd, the forces, under the command of Lord-General Fairfax, had sealed the town off from the outside world completely. There was no possibility of food getting in or any of the residents getting out. This was a harsh decision by the Parliamentary forces, as Colchester had proved itself loyal to Parliament and was not sheltering a Royalist army from choice.

By the beginning of August, people in the town were reduced to eating cats, dogs and then rats. A few weeks later and they were eating candles. Five hundred starving women were sent to the besieging army by the Royalists to beg food. They were stripped naked and sent back again. The siege finally ended in unconditional surrender on August 28th 1648. All the ordinary soldiers were disarmed and allowed to return to their homes, but three of the Royalist commanders were executed by firing squad in the grounds of the castle.

JUNE 14TH

1626: On this day, the first burials of victims of an outbreak of plague in Colchester were buried. We often tend to assume that outbreaks of the plague in England were limited to two or three well-known episodes about which we all learned at school; the Black Death, some time in the Middle Ages and of course the epidemic which swept London in 1665, the year before the Great fire of London. In fact Bubonic Plague was endemic in Europe, including Britain, from the fourteenth century onwards. True, there were serious epidemics and smaller outbreaks, but Europe was never really free of the disease for a number of centuries.

One lesser known flare-up of Bubonic Plague struck Colchester and other parts of Essex in 1626. As usual, the crowded and unsanitary towns were the hardest hit; the larger the town, the higher the mortality. The first victim of the 1626 plague was buried on June 14th 1626. By the end of the year, another seventy-eight people had been died from plague. The authorities were seriously concerned and ordered that the County Gaol be moved from Colchester to Stratford. Justices were also given the power to limit the movement of people and livestock during the emergency.

JUNE 15TH

2009: An archaeological dig ended on this day at East Hill House in Colchester High Street. The house is a Grade I listed eighteenth-century townhouse and some minor renovations were authorised. The Colchester Archaeological Trust were on hand to see what, if anything, might turn up. Since the site was right in the heart of the Roman town, it was not to be wondered that quite a lot of material was unearthed; most of it Roman.

The most significant finds were parts of a hypocaust heating system, which suggested that the house of somebody quite wealthy and important once stood here. Parts of clay flues were found, together with the mortar used to connect them. Some gaming pieces were also found, together with masses of broken pottery from the third century AD. A tessellated floor came to light, which it was supposed might possibly have belonged to a second building. In addition to the Roman material, quite a few odds and ends from later periods turned up, ranging from medieval rubbish to broken clay pipe stems which could have been Victorian.

JUNE 16TH

1381: On this day, disturbances relating to the Peasant's Revolt reached their climax in Colchester. The two main leaders of the revolt, Wat Tyler and the priest John Ball, both seemed to have been associated with Colchester. After the rebellion had been suppressed, one jury described Wat Tyler as being 'of Colchester'. John Ball told listeners that he was 'sometime priest of York and now of Colchester'.

The main thrust of the uprising came from Kent, but a number of men from Colchester and the surrounding villages gathered in the town on June 13th 1381 and headed to London the following day. Two days later, there were disturbances in Colchester itself, with both the Moot Hall and St John's Abbey being attacked by mobs. On the 17th of the same month, rioters carried off goods from the church at Stanway, to the north-east of Colchester. After the failure of the rebellion later in June, several groups of fleeing rebels arrived in Colchester and tried to stir up trouble in the town. Their only success was in provoking resentment against Flemish weavers; there were sporadic attacks on this community for the rest of the year.

JUNE 17TH

2011: Colchester Zoo managed on this day to boost the numbers of its visitors while successfully portraying the day as a charitable venture. No mean feat and the way in which they did this deserves great admiration.

The children's charity Barnado's had arranged a nationwide fundraising initiative called The Big Toddle. Children under the age of 5 would undertake a sponsored walk and this would raise money to be donated to Barnado's. Colchester Zoo issued a press release in which they announced that they would allow toddlers to enter the zoo for nothing, so that they could raise money for, 'supporting children with physical and learning difficulties, autism and behavioural problems'.

The more cynical were quick to note that although the toddlers would be allowed into the zoo for nothing, any adults accompanying them would be charged a tenner a head. True, this was a discount on the usual price, but the zoo calculated, correctly that all those families would be spending money on food, drink and trinkets from their gift shop.

JUNE 18TH

1648: There was on this day a naval engagement in the River Colne. Before the Siege of Colchester began in earnest, the situation was quite fluid. The Royalist army in the town were hoping to receive assistance from other parts of the country. The port of Harwich, for instance, had many supporters of the King's cause and quite a few of these were sailors on ships in the harbour which were nominally under the control of Parliament. At some point, two of these ships mutinied and made their way up the Colne, with a view to attacking the Parliamentary forces from the rear. It was a bold plan and might have succeeded, but for the swift actions of Fairfax; commander of the forces opposing the Royalists at Colchester.

On Mersea Island was a blockhouse, erected in the previous century. This had guns guarding the entrance to the Colne from the sea. It had been in Royalist hands when the ships sailed up the Colne, but soon afterwards, Fairfax sent a small party of dragoons and captured the gun emplacement. All that remained now was for a ship called the *Tiger*, which was loyal to Parliament, to lead a couple of other ships past the now safe blockhouse and up the Colne. The two Royalist frigates surrendered after a brief but bloody battle.

JUNE 19TH

1863: Three cottages and the land surrounding them were bought on this day with the intention of building a Primitive Methodist chapel next to the cottages.

In the early nineteenth century, Primitive Methodism was a powerful evangelical movement with a strong following in Colchester. It was popular among the poorer type of worker in the town. Mainstream Wesleyan Methodism was similar in many ways to the ordinary Anglican Church; John Wesley was, after all, an Anglican minister. Some followers though favoured open-air camp meetings and a more grass roots sort of religion. This led to the two forms of Methodism parting company.

In 1859, the Primitive Methodists in Colchester began to expand outwards, setting up ten chapels in the villages around Colchester. Dedham itself had a well-established Anglican Church and the Methodists decided that rather than compete with this, they would build their chapel in the tiny hamlet of Dedham Heath, a few miles away. They purchased the cottages and adjoining land and, in 1864, the chapel opened for worship.

JUNE 20TH

2011: The *Daily Gazette* reported on this day the plans by Colchester Council to build thirty beach huts at West Mersea. Protestors from the town were bitterly opposed to the proposals.

Essentially, the building of the beach huts, on a patch of grass behind the esplanade, would generate income for Colchester Council. They would each be rented out for £200 or £300 a year and also bring in a total of £2,500 a year in rates. The impetus to build the huts came not from local councillors, but from those living in Colchester itself. Margaret Kimberley, the councillor for West Mersea, however, was quoted as saying:

> These huts will not just have an impact on people living in West Mersea, but the people who visit the island too. They would be built on a very nice, quiet area where people come to relax and children play. The huts would leave less space for that.

West Mersea already has quite a few beach huts, some of which are owned by the council and others by individuals. The privately owned ones change hands for £20,000 or so. Significantly, Colchester Council doubled the rents for the huts which they own recently. The suspicion seemed to be among local residents that they would be priced out of the market for beach huts and that they would all end up being rented to wealthy holidaymakers.

JUNE 21ST

1909: This was the first day of the great Colchester Pageant, which was based in the grounds of Colchester Castle. It was a spectacular event which was intended to celebrate 2,000 years of Colchester's history. The pageant was focused around six important points in the town's history and 3,000 people took part in the tableaux and parades. There were over 200 speaking parts. Each performance lasted three hours, beginning with the dedication of the Temple of Claudius and ending with the Siege of Colchester during the English Civil War.

Music for the pageant, which ran for six days, was specially written by a local schoolmaster. All the costumes were made by local people and after the event these were auctioned for charity. Publicity for the pageant was helped by the then Mayor of Colchester also being the editor of the local newspaper. Special trains were arranged to bring people from London. Some minor members of the Royal family attended and even a visiting party from the Duma; the Russian Parliament. Much of the preparation for the various events during the pageant took place in a private house near the castle. This accordingly became known locally as the 'Pageant House'. Today, we know it better as Hollytrees Museum.

JUNE 22ND

1272: A riot took place on this day between the people living in Colchester and the monks from the Benedictine Abbey of St John's. Tensions between townspeople and those living in abbeys was not at all uncommon in medieval England. The monks enjoyed unusual privileges and those living in the towns and villages had to pay for them. The upkeep of the monasteries was maintained from tithes extracted from the ordinary citizens. Many of these people struggled to make ends meet and it must have sat ill with them to hand over a proportion of their money to the Abbey.

The riot of 1272 took place during the traditional Midsummer Fair. It is impossible to know at this late stage what actually triggered the affair, but it must have been pretty violent. After it was over, a corpse was found near the gates to the abbey and it was claimed that this was in fact a monk who had been killed by the townspeople. This would have been a serious matter, calling for both temporal and divine vengeance. In the event though, it was found that the corpse was not a monk at all. In fact, men from the abbey had crept out under cover of darkness and removed a body from the local gallows. It was this unfortunate that they were trying to pass off as a dead monk!

JUNE 23RD

2001: This day marks the vigil of St John the Baptist in Colchester. Since 2001, this religious day has been marked by a very curious ritual in the town. As part of the Colchester Festival in 2001, a group called the Colchester Town Watch were formed. The local newspaper, the *Colchester Evening Gazette,* contributed to the scheme.

Basically, the Colchester Town Watch are an historical re-enactment society who dress up in armour and Tudor clothing to put on displays around the town. Their uniforms are based upon those of sixteenth-century soldiers and they carry a variety of pikes, swords and so on. On the closest convenient day to July 23rd, the Colchester Town Watch march around the town walls, accompanied by a drummer. The Mayor and Town Crier join in the procession, which terminates at a public house.

Since being founded a little over ten years ago, the Colchester Town Watch has gone from strength to strength. They provide ceremonial guards outside the Town Hall, have public drill sessions, take part in the annual oyster ceremony and also lay wreaths on Remembrance Sunday.

JUNE 24TH

1648: On this day, troops from Suffolk arrived to participate in the Siege of Colchester; more from the desire to protect their own county from harm than any ideological motives.

When a Royalist army turned up at the gates of Colchester in June, the town welcomed them with little enthusiasm. It was clear that their coming would mean nothing but trouble and the sooner they left the better. The Royalists were being pursued by the Parliamentary forces under the command of Lord-General Fairfax. A large body of troops from Suffolk turned up, but showed little interest in taking part in a protracted siege. Instead, their original plan was to head back north and occupy the bridges over the River Stour, which led to their own county.

Fairfax managed to persuade the men from Suffolk that their own best interests would be served by remaining in the vicinity of Colchester and helping him to surround the town. By securing the bridges across the Colne to the north of the town, the Suffolk men could ensure that the Royalists did not break out and rampage towards Suffolk; perhaps seizing Bury St Edmunds or Ipswich as a result.

JUNE 25TH

1786: This is the day that the first Sunday schools opened in Colchester. There were five for boys and seven for girls and they were primarily intended for the children of the poor. This group of Sunday schools were organised by Jonathon Talbot, whose daughter was married to William Fox, founder of the Sunday School Society. Although the main aim of these schools was to encourage children to read the Bible, in many cases this meant first teaching them to read. The motive behind their establishment might have been religious, but the result was really the first schools open to all children.

We are so used to the idea of free education for all, that it comes as something of a shock to remember that in the eighteenth century, few children received any sort of schooling. The churches took the lead by setting about the instruction of children in this way. By the Victorian era, attendance at Sunday school was the rule, rather than the exception for working class children in Colchester, and it is worth remembering the debt which we owe to those early pioneers of free education, who first provided lessons in reading and writing to the children of ordinary workers.

June 26th

1894: The *London Gazette* reported on this day that Weetman Dickinson Pearson was to be granted the title of Baronet; thus becoming Sir Weeton Dickinson Pearson Bt. The following year he was elected as the Liberal MP for Colchester. Fifteen years later, in 1910, he was made Baron Cowdray and in the same year also appointed High Steward of Colchester.

The firm started by Viscount Cowdray's grandfather, Pearson's the publisher, is still going to this day. It is based in Harlow in Essex. During the First World War, Baron Cowdray had an illustrious career, being made firstly a Privy Councillor and then elevated further, from Baron to Viscount Cowdray. The following week, he was made President of the Air Board, with responsibility for the production of military aircraft in Britain.

After the end of the war, Viscount Cowdray devoted himself to philanthropic projects, becoming involved in the Royal Air Force Club and endowing a professorship at Leeds University, among other things. On his death in 1927, his eldest son, Harold, inherited the title of Viscount Cowdray, but the post of High Steward of Colchester was awarded to his widow.

JUNE 27TH

1923: This is the day that Beth Chatto was born. She became Britain's leading plantswoman. In 1960, Beth was living with her husband Andrew near the town of Elmstead Market, which lies a few miles east of Colchester. Part of the land had been a fruit farm, but a large area had never been farmed at all because the soil was very poor. It varied between bleak, dry gravel, heavy clay, and damp, boggy patches. This unpromising location was overgrown with blackthorn, willow and brambles.

Fifty years later, the Beth Chatto Gardens near Colchester are one of the most visited horticultural attractions in the country. The Gravel Garden, Long Shady Walk, Scree Garden and others are each masterpieces of design and planting; showing how even the most unattractive patch of ground may be transformed into a flourishing garden. Little wonder that Beth has won ten consecutive Gold medals at the Chelsea Flower Show.

In addition to her practical work in the garden, Beth is the author of many books on the subject. Their titles are self-explanatory; *The Dry Garden*, *The Damp Garden* and *Beth Chatto's Gravel Garden*, to name but a few. Beth has lectured around the world on the idea of the right plant for the right location. Nobody is better suited to be able to explain this apparently simple principle to aspiring gardeners.

JUNE 28TH

1868: On this day, Joseph Blomfield, managing partner of the Britannia Sewing Machine Company, applied for a patent relating to 'improvements in stands or tables, especially applicable for sewing machines'.

Today, we tend to associate certain large and famous companies with certain household gadgets and sometimes forget that these household names were once only one of many in the field. Hoover, for example, has become synonymous with vacuum cleaners, as has Singer with sewing machines. There was a time though in the nineteenth century when it looked as though the Britannia would become the standard in sewing machines.

Joseph Blomfield was a Colchester ironmonger who had a shop near St Botolph's which sold, among other things, Wheeler and Wilson sewing machines. When the patents on these expired in the late 1860s, Blomfield got together with an engineer called Thomas Bear and they began producing their own sewing machines, which were really pirated copies of the Wheeler and Wilson design. Blomfield dropped all his other business and concerned himself only with sewing machines. In 1871, the company was employing over 100 people and it looked as though they were about to become the major sewing machine manufacturers in Britain. By 1880, though, it was clear that Singer was in the lead and the company switched to making oil engines.

JUNE 29TH

1933: Viscount Ullswater opened the Colchester bypass on this day. At that time, the concept of a road passing round instead of through a city or town was still something of a novelty and so instead of simply being designated by a string of letters or numbers, it was given a name; the Avenue of Remembrance. Trees were planted, with memorial plaques at their bases to those who had died in the First World War.

The building of the Colchester bypass was not without some controversy. The road, which passed south of the town, had the unfortunate effect of separating St Paul's Church from its congregation. In order to reach the church on Sundays, some elderly people now had to cross a busy road.

Fifty years after opening, the bypass suffered the indignity of being itself bypassed! By this time, Colchester had grown and roads had become ten times busier than they had been in 1933. In 1982, the A12 bypass was opened north of Colchester. This meant that it was possible to travel into Suffolk from London on a dual carriageway, without it being necessary to travel at less than 70mph for the entire journey.

JUNE 30TH

2009: On this day, Donald Allison tried to smuggle a rhino horn out of the country through Manchester airport. It is perhaps a little surprising to hear of rhinoceros horns being smuggled *out* of this country; after all, we do not have very much of an indigenous rhinoceros population in England. The explanation was a curious one. In 2009, a rhinoceros called Simba died of natural causes at Colchester Zoo. The corpse was sent to an abattoir for disposal, which was where the rhino's head was sawn off and somehow acquired by Allison, an antiques dealer.

The motive for such an interest in rhino horns is purely financial. The market value in China of white rhino horn is around £60,000 per kilo; roughly twice as much as platinum or gold. It is an integral part of various traditional Chinese medicines and very hard to get hold of these days. The problem with somebody selling the horn of a rhinoceros is that it promotes the trade and encourages poaching in Africa. Colchester Zoo recently fitted an alarm system in their rhino enclosure to detect and deter any poaching.

In October 2010, Donald Allison was sent to prison for a year for attempting to smuggle an endangered species.

JULY 1ST

1963: On this day, the lifeboat station at West Mersea opened. Mersea is one of those places of which many have heard, but few are able to pinpoint with any accuracy. This is odd, because Mersea should be famous as the most easterly inhabited island of the British isles.

Mersea Island lies at the mouth of the Colne and Blackwater rivers. It is in the borough of Colchester and was formerly known as Mersey Island. Mersea covers an area of just seven square miles and has a population of around 7,000, mostly living in two settlements; East and West Mersea. The island is connected to the mainland by a causeway known as the Strood, which is often flooded at high tide.

Mersea Island has been inhabited since before the Roman Invasion. The red hills on the island are evidence of Celtic salt workings and Roman mosaics have also been uncovered there. Today, the main industries are farming and fishing. Although technically an island, the communities on Mersea enjoy all the modern amenities to be found on the mainland, including broadband access. There is a primary school, but once they reach the age of 11, children are obliged to travel nine miles to Colchester for their secondary education.

JULY 2ND

1849: The first train ran across Chappel Viaduct on this day. The Chappel Viaduct runs across a section of the Colne Valley, near the village of Chappel in the borough of Colchester. The viaduct is an awe-inspiring sight; a magnificent legacy of the early Victorian railway age. It is the second largest brick structure in Britain, with only Battersea power station using more bricks in its construction.

The Chappel Viaduct has a number of remarkable features. To begin with, it took two years to build and the workers and their families moved into a kind of shanty town on Wakes Colne Green while it was being built. It is over 1,000 feet long, with a maximum height of 75 feet. It has been calculated that six million bricks were used to build the viaduct, which carries the line from Marks Tey to Sudbury. The thirty-two piers are hollow, to make them lighter. A very unusual feature about this viaduct is that it rises in a gradient: the Sudbury end is almost 10 feet higher than the Marks Tey end.

Peter Bruff, the railway engineer responsible for planning the Chappel Viaduct, chose to build it in brick, rather than constructing it from wood. This was not, as might be thought, so that it would last longer, but because brick worked out cheaper than using laminated wood; the material originally suggested.

JULY 3RD

1938: On this day, the *Essex County Standard* carried the obituary of Frederick Isaac English.

Frederick was born in Colchester in 1890. When war broke out between England and Germany on August 4th 1914, English was swift to join up. He went with the British Expeditionary Force to France, thus earning himself the title accorded by the Kaiser of belonging to 'this contemptible little army'. The term 'Old Contemptible' was adopted proudly by the survivors of this military expedition.

It was something of a miracle that Frederick survived the war. He was wounded five times and gassed twice. The gas wrecked his health and he never really recovered. He was awarded the Distinguished Conduct Medal by Britain and the *Medaille Militaire* by France. He ended the war as an acting Sergeant in the 1st King's Royal Rifles. When he died at the age of 48, his funeral service was held at Lexden Methodist Church and he was buried in Lexden churchyard.

JULY 4TH

1953: Jess Jephcott, who set up the Camulos website, was born in Barnet General Hospital on this day. When he was 2, his family moved to Walton-on-the-Naze and then, when he was a teenager, he moved to Colchester, where he has lived ever since.

The Camulos website was set up in 1999 and for anybody with even the slightest interest in Colchester and its history, it is invaluable. Information is to be found there on every conceivable aspect of the town over the millennia. Whether you are interested in the Roman city or wish to know something about the backgrounds of those buried in Colchester Cemetery, if you want to know more about Colchester's churches or learn about famous businesses which have been based there; the Camulos website should be your first port of call. The website is constantly being updated and if you can't find what you wish to know this week, it may very well be on there the next.

JULY 5TH

1621: On this day, Thomas Darcy was created 1st Viscount Colchester. The Darcy family have had quite a history in Colchester. In 1539, the abbey of St John's at Colchester was suppressed by Henry VIII at the beginning of the English Reformation. The Abbot refused to go quietly and was eventually hanged for treason. The abbey itself passed to the Crown and in 1546 was leased to one Sir Thomas Darcy. It was this man's son, born in 1565, who became the 1st Viscount Colchester.

The Darcy family appear to have been swamped with various honours and titles, to the extent that it is almost impossible to disentangle who was what. The Thomas Darcy who was created 1st Viscount Colchester was already 3rd Baron Darcy of Chiche and, five years after being made Viscount Colchester, was created Earl Rivers. The title of Viscount Colchester was later somehow passed to his son-in-law. An instrument was drawn up which arranged for:

> The reversion to Thomas Savage, Knight and Baronet, one of the Gentlemen of the Chamber, husband of Elizabeth, daughter of Lord Darcy and to the heirs male of his body by the said Elizabeth.

July 6th

1428: A 6-year-old King Henry VI wrote to the Governors of Colchester on this day:

> Be it known to you that, perfectly relying upon your fidelity and prudence, we have charged you, both together and separately, to arrest and apprehend William White and all others suspected of heresy and to send them, as soon as you have apprehended them, to our nearest jails or prisons, until we have given orders for their release.

Of course, it is not really to be supposed that the 6-year-old King actually wrote these words himself. There was a serious outbreak of heresy in Colchester at this time, led by three former priests. It was considered essential that these dangerous men should be caught as soon as possible; the country not being prepared to reject the Catholic Church for another century or so. When they were captured, all the heretics were burned at the stake in Colchester.

JULY 7TH

2009: The body of Graham Reeve was found on this day at his home in Charles Pell Road, Colchester. The 55-year-old man had been tortured over a period of several hours, before finally being murdered. The motive for this horrific crime was almost unbelievably trivial. Two men had attacked Graham Reeve as he was returning to his home on the Greenstead Estate. They then held him captive in his own home while they tried to force him to reveal the PIN number for his bank card.

Danny Housego, 36, and Jon Williams, 22, were subsequently convicted of the murder of Mr Reeves. Although unable to persuade him to give them the PIN for his card, the pair managed to use it in a supermarket to order £250-worth of alcohol and food, which they had delivered to the address where they were holding the card's owner. Eventually, they strangled him with a piece of cord. After they were both convicted at Chelmsford Crown Court, they were sentenced to life imprisonment, with a recommendation by the judge that they should each serve at least thirty-two years in prison before being considered for parole.

JULY 8TH

2010: Sam Moorhead from the Portable Antiquities Scheme visited Colchester Metal Detecting Club on this day. The Portable Antiquities Scheme (PAS) was set up in conjunction with museums to try to ensure that coins, jewellery and other archaeological remains which are small enough to pick up and carry home are recorded and the locations where they were found made known to professional archaeologists.

Those whose hobby is metal detecting have in the past been eyed a little askance by traditional archaeology. This is largely due to the activities of the so-called 'night hawks', who raid sites under the cover of darkness looking for treasure. The aim of the talk given to the Colchester metal detectorists was to emphasise the importance of even badly worn or corroded coins in building up an accurate picture of the ancient past. By recording the location where these have been found, clues might build up as to the whereabouts of smaller settlements whose location has been forgotten over the centuries.

JULY 9TH

1635: On this day, the post of High Steward of Colchester was established by a royal charter of Charles I. The charter, which was directed by name to all the officials of the town, said that:

> Henceforth forever there may be and shall be in the borough a High Steward to advise and direct the Mayor and Commonality in the chief business touching that borough which High Steward shall continue in that office of High Steward during his natural life.

At one time the post of High Steward had a considerable amount of power associated with it, but this declined markedly after the Civil War. In 1835, the Municipal Corporation Act replaced town corporations with elected councils. Nearly all High Stewards were abolished at this time, except in the case of a couple of dozen towns, Colchester among them, which petitioned to retain their High Stewards. A condition of allowing the retention of the post was that the charters establishing them should be amended so that from 1836 onwards, the stewards should only be able 'to advise' rather than 'to advise and direct'. Twenty-four other towns and districts still have High Stewards, although in some of these the post has fallen into abeyance. Notable High Stewards include Prince Philip, Lord High Steward of Plymouth, and the Duke of Kent, High Steward of King's Lynn and West Norfolk.

July 10th

1997: Nelson Mandela visited the University of Essex on this day, when his wife, Graca Machel, received an honorary degree in recognition of her work for the rights of children. During the course of his speech, Mandela said, 'This is a very famous university which has been involved in the fight for human rights in all parts of the world'. This was a reference to the university's Human Rights Centre, which was established in 1982 by Professor David Yates. It is part of the university's Law Department and its first director was Dr Malcolm Shaw.

In 1989, the centre was revamped and it became possible to study there for an MA in the Theory and Practice of Human Rights. The staff consist of lawyers, philosophers and political theorists, all of whom have one thing in common; a passionate commitment to the upholding of human rights throughout the world. The staff have had practical experience in the field of human rights, working with such agencies as the United Nations and Amnesty International. With its programme of teaching and research, the centre has a worldwide reputation.

July 11th

2008: On this day, the Colchester Morris Men performed in front of the Bricklayers' Arms public house in Little Bentley, Essex; which performance was filmed and is available to view on YouTube.

The Colchester Morris Dancing Club was formed in 1926, but then fell into abeyance during the years of the Second World War from 1939 to 1945. It was reformed in 1953 and has been going strong ever since. They dance outside from May to September and also have a tradition of dancing outside the Black Buoy in Wivenhoe on Boxing Day.

There are different types of Morris Dancing. The Colchester group tend to concentrate mainly on the Cotswold tradition, with a bit of border dancing thrown in. They dance to the music of accordions, violins, pipes and tabors and each session lasts approximately three quarters of an hour. Their activities are not limited to Essex; in August they dance in Norfolk and in September they find time to visit Suffolk. During border dancing, they black up their faces, which has in the past led to accusations of racism. These are based upon the incorrect assumption that the blacking of faces is done in mockery of black people. In fact, it was an old way of concealing the identity of the dancers.

JULY 12TH

1913: At 1 p.m. on this day, two trains collided at Colchester railway station.

The express from Cromer to London passed through Colchester station without stopping or even slowing down. The signal indicated that the line ahead was clear and the driver of the train could not have guessed that the man in the signal box had simply pressed the wrong key and should have ordered the express to stop. On the line ahead was a small engine used for shunting and it was pootling along very slowly, right in the path of the oncoming express train. There were three men in the cab of the express train; the driver, fireman and an inspector. The drive and fireman were killed instantly, as was the guard in the van at the rear of the train. The driver of the other locomotive survived, although with serious injuries. No passengers were killed, although one was still in hospital a month later.

In August 1913, Lieutenant-Colonel Von Donop prepared a report on the accident for the Board of Trade. Since the driver of the Cromer to London express was really the one who should have been keeping a better lookout and he was now dead, the report did not lead to any further action.

JULY 13TH

1936: Ron Beecham was born on this day. Between 1972 and 1975 he was Chair of the National Accordion Association and established the Accordion School in Colchester. He formed the Colchester Accordion Orchestra, which travelled the world, gathering prizes and bringing honour to the name of Colchester.

The accordion is not perhaps the most well-known musical instrument. In Colchester though, it is big part of the music scene. This is largely due to the efforts of Ron Beecham and his wife Elaine. Following her husband's death in 2006, Elaine Beecham has continued to keep accordion playing in the forefront of the minds of Colchester's residents.

A brief glance at the Accordions Unlimited website will soon convince people that no musical instrument has more of a history in Colchester than the accordion. Indeed, the Colchester Accordion orchestra was even granted the honour of using the town's crest, 'when the orchestra won a GOLD MEDAL in the WORLD BAND CHAMPIONSHIP' [*sic*]. Such dedication has not gone unnoticed. Elaine Beecham was awarded the National Merit Award in 2002, 'for devoted service to the accordion'.

JULY 14TH

1648: An event which happened on this day led to the writing of one of our most popular nursery rhymes. We are most of us familiar with the words of 'Humpty Dumpty':

> Humpty Dumpty sat on a wall,
> Humpty Dumpty had a great fall,
> All the King's horses and all the King's men,
> Couldn't put Humpty together again.

Humpty Dumpty was in fact the nickname of an enormous, bulbous cannon used by the Royalist forces in the defence of Colchester when the town was besieged by the Parliamentary army. The cannon was hoisted onto the city wall near St Mary's Church, where it had a perfect field of fire against the opposing forces.

On July 14th, the cannons of General Fairfax's forces began targeting the stretch of wall upon which Humpty Dumpty had been set. Eventually, it collapsed and the great cannon crashed to the ground, where it shattered into pieces. All the 'King's men', that is to say the Royalist soldiers, were indeed unable to put Humpty together again!

It is only fair to say that there is another explanation for the origin of the nursery rhyme; one which also involves the Siege of Colchester. A Royalist sniper called 'One-Eyed Thompson' was positioned in the belfry of St Mary's and was eventually brought down by gunfire from the Parliamentary soldiers. According to this version, it was Thompson who was nicknamed 'Humpty Dumpty'.

JULY 15TH

1648: This day saw the start of three days of fierce fighting, which became known as the Battle of Boxted Heath. Essex had in general been solidly behind Parliament during the early years of the English Civil War. By 1648 though, the Royalists were finding some support in the county. After the Siege of Colchester had lasted for a month or so, some of the Royalists holding the town decided that it was time to take the fight to the enemy. About 1,000 cavalry sallied forth on July 15th and engaged Fairfax's army at Boxted, some miles north of Colchester. For three days and nights, the opposing forces fought in a desultory and indecisive fashion, until the Royalists had had enough. A contemporary account of the fighting tells what happened:

> This evening all the gentlemen volunteers, with all the horse of the garrison, with Sir Charles Lucas, Sir George Lisle and Sir Bernard Gascoigne at the head of them resolved to break through the enemy and forcing a pass to advance into Suffolk by Nayland Bridge; to this purpose they passed the river near Middle-Mill, but their guides having misled them the enemy took the alarm, upon which their guides and some pioneers which they had with them . . . all ran away, so the horse were obliged to retreat, the enemy pretended to pursue, but thinking they had retired by North Bridge, they missed them, upon which, being enraged, they fired the suburbs without the bridge, and burned them quite down.

On July 18th, they fought a ferocious rearguard action and returned to Colchester.

July 16th

1875: The *Essex Standard* reported on this day that the person responsible for the Fordham murders had been committed to the Criminal Lunatic Asylum at Broadmoor.

On March 20th 1875, Thomas Johnson beat to death his parents; his father was 81 and his mother 79. The murder took place at Fordham, a village near Colchester. Johnson made no attempt to escape and was soon arrested. He told the first people whom he met after the murder that he was God Almighty. He made the same claim to the police constable who took him into custody. During the preliminary examination in the magistrate's court, Johnson showed little interest in the proceedings, beyond mentioning in passing that his parents had bewitched him. When the hearing was over and he had been formally charged with the murder of his parents, he was asked if he wished to make a statement. He said in an agitated voice:

It is quite true. I want to destroy the Devil's kingdom and build up God Almighty's. Do you wish me to say any more?

There was little more that could be said and, under the circumstances, it can hardly have come as any surprise that when he appeared in court at Chelmsford four months later, he was found to be unfit to plead.

July 17th

924: Edward the Elder died on this day. He was the son of Alfred the Great and responsible for liberating Colchester from foreign rule. In AD 865, the Vikings invaded eastern England and over the course of the next four or five years, occupied it. They established a Danish realm from London in the south to York in the north, which included the whole of East Anglia. This area became known as the Danelaw. Alfred the Great prevented further expansion of the Vikings, and his son Edward, known as Edward the Elder, led the counter-attack; liberating the whole country from the Danish yoke.

There are many Danish place names to be found in much of East Anglia; Norfolk, Suffolk and Lincolnshire are rich in such names. In Essex, only a few are to be found and these are clustered around Colchester: Kirby-le-Soken and Thorpe-le-Soken are good examples. Colchester made an excellent base for the seafaring Vikings. It had direct access to the sea via the River Colne and at that time its Roman walls were almost intact, making it a brilliantly defensible position.

The Viking occupation of Colchester lasted for a little over fifty years. In AD 921, Edward the Elder led his armies to the town and drove out the Danish invaders. In the words of the *Anglo-Saxon Chronicle*, his army, 'went to Colchester and beset the town and fought thereon until they took it and slew all the people and seized all that was therein; except those men who escaped therefrom by jumping over the wall'.

JULY 18TH

1905: Francis Cowper died on this day. He was High Steward of Colchester at his death, but this was only one of many honours which had been conferred upon him.

When he was born in 1834, he was the 7th Earl Cowper. From 1837 to 1856 though, he was known as Viscount Fordwich. He entered the House of Lords upon the death of his father and was soon made Captain of the Honourable Corps of Men-at-Arms; Government Chief Whip in ordinary language. He became a Knight of the Garter in 1865 and Lord Lieutenant of Ireland from 1880 to 1882. In 1883, he became High Steward of Colchester. He was also High Lieutenant of Bedfordshire and Deputy Lieutenant of Nottinghamshire and Kent. Some nifty legal wrangling enabled him to pursue a claim to the Lordship of Dingwall in Scotland, thus becoming 4th Lord Dingwall. When his mother died, he inherited another title from her and was thereafter the 8th Baron Lucas of Crudwell.

July 19th

1988: On this day, the beacon in Castle Park was first lit by Mayor Graham Bober. It had been erected as a permanent structure in order to commemorate the defeat of the Spanish Armada in 1588. A stout wooden pillar is topped by a crown-shaped brazier, which can be filled with combustible material. It has been contrived to look self-consciously antique; which for a municipal monument is not at all surprising.

Considering the solidity of the beacon and the evident intention to make something which would last, the subsequent use of the thing has been sparing in the extreme. Eleven years after the lighting of the fire to celebrate the 400th anniversary of the Armada's defeat, Mayor Martin Hunt signalled the end of the old millennium and beginning of the new by lighting another fire in the beacon on December 31st 1999. Then, a few years later, Mayor Terry Sutton lit another fire to mark Trafalgar Day on October 21st 2005. Since that day, the beacon has remained unused. It is to be hoped that Colchester Borough Council will come up with some more notable days to celebrate in this way.

JULY 20TH

1960: The last secondary pupils at Mersea Island finished their education on this day. From then on, pupils would have to travel to Colchester for their secondary education.

Until the 1944 Education Act, most children in this country attended all-age elementary schools. These catered for children from the age of 5 to 14, when 90 per cent of children left school. This meant that rural communities like Mersea needed only one school. After the Second World War, secondary education was provided free and made compulsory for all children up to the age of 15. Prior to this, only those whose parents could afford to pay school fees went to secondary school. Even grammar schools were only for those whose parents could afford them, although scholarships were available for some.

Changing the law did not alter the fact that most school buildings were still geared to the elementary school system and things did not change overnight. Well into the 1950s, there were still quite a number of elementary schools still operating. The only difference now was that the children stayed there until 15, rather than 14. It was still not secondary education, though, and great efforts were made to ensure that every child in Britain attended a proper secondary school after the age of 11. Mersea was one of the last places to achieve this.

JULY 21ST

1835: On this day, Beau Brummell, the famous dandy, was released from a debtors prison in France. His notoriously extravagant lifestyle and taste for ostentatious clothes had driven him into debt in Britain, forcing him to flee abroad. If only he had followed the example of his older brother, William.

William Brummell had inherited about the same amount as George Bryant, Beau's real name, on the death of their father in 1794. Instead of squandering it on fancy clothes and silver spittoons, however, he had bought a comfortable house in Essex.

While his younger brother had been living beyond his means and ended up in a debtors' prison, William had a handsome house built in Wivenhoe. Wivenhoe House stood to the east of the High Road and was a restrained but imposing edifice of white brick. William lived quietly and respectably here until his death in 1853. It was, by the standards of the time, a fairly modest establishment for a wealthy man. William and his wife Ann lived there, with their two daughters and seven servants. His wife died four years later, after which the estate was broken up and sold off for building plots.

JULY 22ND

1342: This day marked the final day of what was virtually a Siege of Colchester lasting two months. During the thirteenth and fourteenth centuries, there were many civil disturbances, not just in Essex, but throughout the entire country. Sometimes, these degenerated into what were essentially civil wars; at others, it was more a question of rioting. The affair at Colchester in 1342 fell somewhere between these two extremes.

There had for many years been friction between the noble family of FitzWalter, who had estates at Lexden, and the citizens of Colchester. At various times, Lord FitzWalter accused the men of Colchester of poaching on his land and stealing from his servants. Matters came to a head when one of his servants was attacked to the north of Colchester and died of his injuries. Lord FitzWalter blamed the people of Colchester for this death and when the inquest held in the town failed to deliver what he saw as the correct verdict, he ordered his men to surround the town and prevent anybody leaving. It was not a very effective siege and largely consisted of Lord FitzWalter's men roughing up and mugging people as they left the town. In the end, after two months of increasing tension, the townspeople bought off the Lord by paying him £40 compensation for the loss of his servant; whereupon business returned to normal.

JULY 23RD

2011: The economic crisis which gripped the country caused the Colchester Tattoo to be cancelled; it was originally to be held on this day. When it was held in 2009, the festival attracted over 30,000 people. Announcing the cancellation, Colonel Tom Fleetwood, Commander of the Colchester Garrison, was quoted as saying that given the current pressure of budgets, he could not justify a case for holding the event.

The Colchester Tattoo is more than a chance to show off the army's military equipment. It has, over the years, raised thousands of pounds for various charities, including the Army Benevolent Fund. Major Peter Harcle of the Army Benevolent Fund said:

> The spending cuts have been forced on the army like everybody else and they've had to make some tough decisions. In the past, the proceeds of the festival have been split between different charities and on average we got £6,600 to £8,000 each time

This was the second year that the Colchester Tattoo was cancelled. In 2010, it was unable to go ahead because of the overseas commitments of the armed forces.

JULY 24TH

2011: This is the day that The Great British Circus left Colchester after a five-day stay. The Great British Circus is the only touring circus in the entire country which still has big cats. A typical show consists of a ringmaster getting tigers and lions to jump through hoops and sit up and beg. The big tent was pitched at London Road, Stanway; not far from Colchester Zoo.

In 2005, a campaign by a group of vegetarians and animal rights activists was organised to try and prevent the circus from coming to town. When it visited, crowds of demonstrators gathered to jeer at families coming to watch the show. The police were called, but since there was no violence or intimidation, did nothing. On that occasion, the big top, which can seat 500 people, was half empty.

Part of the animal rights campaigners' aim was to encourage people to complain to those who rented out their land for the use of the circus. The circus went ahead, despite a few protestors.

July 25th

1645: Fourteen women convicted of witchcraft were hanged in Chelmsford on this day. They were victims of Matthew Hopkins, the self-styled Witchfinder General, and had previously been detained in cells at Colchester Castle.

Essex was long known as the 'witch county'. When witch-hunting fever took hold in England in the middle of the seventeenth century, it was not at all surprising that it should be East Anglia in general and Essex in particular which should be the main target for the witch hunts. Hopkins had been a lawyer's clerk and innkeeper before the start of the English Civil War. With the ensuing chaos, he perhaps saw an opportunity to make something more of himself.

In March 1645, Hopkins teamed up with a man called John Stearne and together they managed to persuade a local magistrate to commission them to question a suspected witch called Elizabeth Clarke. This case turned into something of a bonanza for the witch hunters, because Clarke confessed and also implicated a number of other supposed witches. Eventually, thirty-three of them were held in Colchester Castle in appalling conditions. In addition to the fourteen hanged in Chelmsford, four were taken to Manningtree to be hanged. Those who cooperated were released.

July 26th

1553: On this day, Queen Mary visited Colchester and was presented with a silver cup. When her brother, Edward VI, died, there was some doubt about whether Mary would accede to the throne. She went to East Anglia, where support for her was strong. At Framlingham in Suffolk, she coordinated her plans to seize the throne. On July 10th, she was declared Queen and prepared to enter the capital. The citizens of Colchester had already sent supplies to Framlingham, which included barrels of beer and sides of beef.

Mary's visit to Colchester was by way of being part of a triumphal tour of her kingdom before she was crowned. While she was in the town, she was given, in a addition to the silver cup, £20 in gold and enough provisions to feed her retainers as they made their way to London. It was a canny move to ingratiate themselves with the new monarch. Her first actions on reaching London on August 3rd were to start settling scores with those she suspected of disloyalty. By inviting her to stay and giving so much of their produce to the new Queen, Colchester at least had proved its loyalty.

JULY 27TH

1889: On this day James Morris Colquhoun Colvin joined the Royal Engineers. The army was to be his life. It was in a campaign in North West India, near to where the present day Afghan war is being fought, that Colvin won that most coveted of British medals; the Victoria Cross.

On the night of September 16th 1897, Colvin was part of a unit who were attempting to clear a village of enemy troops. The village caught fire and the men around him were wounded, yet Colvin continued fighting throughout the entire night. The flames meant that he was visible to the enemy for the whole time. Over the following decades, Colvin was mentioned in despatches and fought in the First World War, by the end of which he had risen to the rank of Lieutenant-Colonel.

On his retirement from the army, Colvin settled in Stanway, near Colchester. He was destined to live long enough to see an even more ferocious war than the one in which he had last seen service. He lived through the whole of the Second World War, dying in Stanway on December 7th 1945.

JULY 28TH

1904: On this day Colchester Corporation began operating trams in the town. Since Colchester at that time was a fairly small town, the need for trams requires some explanation. When the railway came to Colchester in the 1840s, the awkward topography of the town and the position of the River Colne meant that the station was built some distance from the town itself. Some years later, another and more convenient station was built, but the main station on the line from London was always destined to be a little out of the way.

For a while, horse-drawn wagons plied for trade to carry passengers from the station to the centre of Colchester, but in 1904 the corporation opened the tram system, which was really geared around the stations. It lasted only twenty-five years. By the late 1920s, it was clear that petrol-driven vehicles were the future and the trams were replaced by a fleet of buses.

JULY 29TH

1847: John Gurdon Rebow stood unsuccessfully for North Essex at the General Election, which began on this day. In those days, elections lasted for a week, which is how long it took to count all the votes throughout the country and then convey the results to London. Despite his failure to get into Parliament, Rebow held a number of important positions, including, from 1861, the post of High Steward of Colchester. Before this he was variously a JP, Deputy Lieutenant, and then High Sheriff of Essex.

In February 1857, Rebow stood for Parliament again and this time he was elected as the MP for Colchester. Two years later, he was defeated again, but then regained the seat at the election in 1865. This time, he remained Colchester's MP until his death in 1870. John Gurdon Rebow had many connections with the Colchester area, not least by his marriage to Mary Ormsby, who was living at Wivenhoe Park. He was living at Wivenhoe Park, a grand house with a large estate surrounding it, when he was elected in 1865 and remained there until his death.

JULY 30TH

1863: The new Congregational Church in Lion Walk, Colchester opened on this day. Colchester has always had a strong nonconformist community and until 1863, the congregation in Lion Walk met in a plain, octagonal Meeting House; very similar to a Quaker place of worship. Things changed when the 24-year-old Revd Davids arrived to be their pastor. The congregation increased exponentially, to the point where an astounding 1,000 children were attending the Sunday school. Such a large congregation required a larger church and a new one was built of Caen stone in the Victorian Gothic style. Some members of the congregation left in disgust, claiming that the new church looked more Catholic than Congregationalist.

Local people in Colchester christened the new church St David's Cathedral and, once the novelty had worn off, it soon became an accepted landmark in the town centre. Over the years, however, the stone began to deteriorate and the cost of rebuilding it was beyond the financial abilities of the church. A happy compromise was reached with a property developer and the body of the church was demolished and a new church built above a shopping centre. The tower and spire remain though; St David's Cathedral has not altogether vanished.

JULY 31ST

2007: Two boys, one 16 and the other just 13, were arrested this day for the rape and murder of a 24-year-old mother. Helen Maughan had been drinking in the pubs of central Colchester when she ran into the two boys. They had been drinking wine and strong lager for most of the day and their version of what happened is that the young woman sat down with them and asked to share their alcohol. Since she had been refused service in three pubs that day, because she was drunk, this is entirely possible. By one of the boys' account, she then tried to kiss him and the other boy grew jealous. A row then erupted and she was accidentally killed. Her body was then dumped in the nearby River Colne.

When the case came to court, a grimmer picture emerged of the dead woman's last moments. A pathologist found no fewer than twenty-two injuries to her genitals and face. She had been raped and savagely beaten, before being thrown in the river. She had still been alive at this point and she died of drowning. The older of the two boys was subsequently found guilty of murder and sentenced to at least fifteen years in prison. The younger boy received four years for manslaughter.

AUGUST 1ST

10 BC: Claudius, the Roman emperor, was born on this day. He became emperor in AD 41 almost by accident after the assassination of his nephew, Caligula. The army regarded him as being a weak and relatively harmless candidate for the throne. As a result of this, Claudius spent the rest of his life proving that he was a strong leader. His conquest of Britain in AD 43 was an example of this desperate need to assert himself.

After Claudius' death in AD 54, he was deified; that is to say declared a god. A huge temple was built in Colchester, dedicated to the worship of the late emperor. This temple, paid for by and constructed by the labour of the conquered Britons, provided the spark which led to Boudicca's uprising and the destruction of the whole city of Colchester. This vulgar and ostentatious building offended the religious sensibilities of those living in the former city of Camulodunum, especially since many of their homes were destroyed to make room for it. When Boudicca torched the town in AD 60, the terrified Roman colonists took shelter in the temple. They were all massacred. The foundations of the temple were still visible a thousand years later during the Norman Conquest, and the Normans built their castle upon them. It is possible today to visit the vaults of the temple, deep beneath Colchester Castle.

AUGUST 2ND

1557: This is the day that ten people were burned alive in Colchester, victims of the so-called Marian Persecutions which took place under Queen Mary. After the death of Henry VIII and the brief reign of his son, Edward VI, the throne passed to Henry's older daughter, Mary. She was a devout Catholic who was determined to reverse the reformation of the Church instituted by he father. She chose to accomplish this end by encouraging the courts to try for heresy those who had drifted from the Catholic fold.

Among those who fell foul of the new regime was William Munt, a Colchester man who refused to attend a Catholic church. In 1557 he was arrested, along with his wife Alice and daughter Rose. The family were taken to Colchester Castle, which at that time was being used as a prison. A man called John Johnson was arrested at the same time and also lodged in the castle. Six others who were detained during raids were imprisoned in other parts of the county.

All ten of the prisoners were convicted of heresy and sentenced to be burned alive. The first batch were disposed of on the morning of August 2nd, when they were shackled to posts outside Colchester and a fierce fire built around them. In the afternoon, it was the turn of John Johnson and the Munt family. Rose Munt was only a teenager, but she still refused to recant and attend a Catholic church. They were burned at the stake in the grounds of Colchester Castle and by all accounts suffered this hideous death with great bravery.

AUGUST 3RD

1912: This day saw the first recorded flight of an aeroplane from Colchester. Southend-on-Sea is well known today for its air shows, but the very first was held two years before the start of the First World War. On August Bank Holiday Monday, Monsieur M. Salmet took off from Colchester and headed thirty-two miles south to Southend. He had landed at Colchester in his fragile-looking aeroplane the day before.

Upon reaching Southend, Salmet gave an amazing display of aerobatics, swooping down within a few feet of the sea and even looping the loop; no mean feat in such a primitive machine. The beach and pier were crowded with onlookers and the daring pilot remarked later that he had never seen so many people in one place.

When he ended the exhibition and landed at Priory Farm Meadow, Monsieur Salmet was mobbed by excited young women clamouring for his autograph. Aeroplanes had been around for less than a decade and this was the first ever seen in Southend. His progress to the Palace Hotel, where a room had been booked for him, was like a triumphal tour through the streets.

AUGUST 4TH

2008: The first football match played by Colchester United FC in their new home ground, the Colchester Community Stadium, was played on this day. Colchester United lost the game 2-1 to Athletic Bilbao. The stadium, known also as Weston Homes Community Stadium, cost £14 million to build. Colchester Borough Council and Colchester United Football Club put up the bulk of this, with other funding coming from the Football Foundation and The East of England Development Agency. Soon after the stadium was completed, Colchester United FC revealed that they had struck a £2 million sponsorship deal with Weston Homes, whereby the stadium would be named after the company, who would also have their logo on the team's shirts for the first two seasons.

The stadium has a capacity of 10,000 and parking for 600 vehicles. There is space to increase the capacity from 10,000 to 18,000. There is some reason to suppose that this might be necessary in the future, as more than one game has been played to a full stadium. On January 10th 2010, for instance, a crowd of 10,064 watched Colchester United lose 5-0 to Norwich.

AUGUST 5TH

2011: One-hundred-and-six-year-old Leslie Dunn was fitted with a pacemaker on this day at Colchester General Hospital. Mr Dunn had been brought to the hospital after collapsing while making a cup of tea. It was found that his heart was beating irregularly and so the decision was taken to fit a pacemaker. The oldest patient previously fitted with a pacemaker at Colchester General had been 101.

The operation to fit the pacemaker was carried out under local anaesthetic by registrar Iqbal Toor. Although not the oldest person in this country to be fitted with a pacemaker – that distinction belongs to a 107-year-old man in Scotland – Mr Dunn's case was still extraordinary. A former professional soldier, Mr Dunn retired from the Coldstream Guards in 1956; in other words, when he had the pacemaker fitted, he had been retired for fifty-five years! Incredibly, he still lived by himself in a second-floor flat and fully intended on leaving hospital to return to his independent lifestyle.

AUGUST 6TH

1445: Henry VI visited Colchester on this day, when he was 24. He was accompanied by his new Queen, Margaret of Anjou. Although she had only just turned 15 when they married, she proved in the long run to have the stronger character.

Henry and Margaret's visit to Colchester, just four and a half months after the wedding, was intended as a tour of his realm and an opportunity to show his wife the country. The marriage had not been a popular one and there were already the mutterings of discontent which were to become the Wars of the Roses; a full-scale civil war. One of the causes of anger was that part of the marriage settlement consisted of England's possessions of the lands around Anjou and Maine in France.

For the next few years, Henry VI maintained his grip on power, but his wife showed herself to be an avaricious and grasping woman. In 1447, for instance, she somehow persuaded her husband to give her Colchester Castle as an outright gift. This sort of thing made it seem as though she were preparing something of a power base.

AUGUST 7TH

1984: There were scuffles at Wivenhoe port on this day as attempts were made to break the miners' strike by importing coal from abroad. Wivenhoe came to symbolise the conflict between a union and the government determined to defeat it.

There were large stockpiles of coal at the beginning of the 1984/5 miners' strike; certainly enough to last for months. Nevertheless, the government had to plan for the possibility of a protracted strike, which is in fact what happened. One way of mitigating the effects of the stoppage by the mine workers was to bring in coal from other countries. The problem was that the main ports of Britain, places like Liverpool, were famous for their militant union activity. Any attempt to move coal through them would probably have triggered strikes by workers there as well. The last thing the government wanted was a wave of strikes in other industries in support of the miners. The plan was therefore to bring the coal in through smaller ports, where there was no tradition of left wing activism. Wivenhoe seemed perfect for this purpose.

Miners from Kent turned up to picket Wivenhoe and found themselves facing lines of police. Inevitably, there was confrontation which sometimes degenerated into violence.

AUGUST 8TH

2010: The *Chelmsford Weekly News* reported on this day that the previous week had seen a spate of sightings of UFOs in the skies above Colchester. The statements of witnesses suggested that identifying these particular flying object was not likely to prove too difficult.

Steve Woods, for instance, saw something in the sky which was moving with the prevailing wind. He said, 'it looked like a big balloon'. Later that day, another Colchester resident saw something which looked 'twice as big as the sun and fiery on all the edges'.

When we see something which looks like a big balloon, then the most likely explanation is probably the correct one; in short, it probably *was* a balloon. Chinese lanterns are small hot air balloons powered by tea lights and popularly released at events ranging from weddings to funerals. They rise into the air and frequently end up catching fire and crashing to the ground. They have become such a scourge that many farmers now complain of their ability to start fires in dry fields. Since they became popular, reports of UFOs have soared across the entire country.

AUGUST 9TH

1923: Lexden Tumulus was scheduled as an ancient monument on this day. The Lexden Tumulus is a late Iron-Age burial mound on the outskirts of Colchester. It is of an extremely unusual design for the period, being circular. This style went out of fashion a thousand years or so before the Lexden Tumulus was raised over the cremated remains of some notable individual. The tumulus contained the richest Iron-Age burial ever excavated in Britain. It can be dated fairly accurately by the so-called Lexden medallion – a silver pendent made from a cast of a Roman coin which dated from 18-16 BC. Clearly, the grave cannot have been constructed any earlier than this.

In its way, the contents of the Lexden Tumulus were as exciting as those found in Tutankhamun's tomb: amphorae from Italy, chain mail, bronze ornaments and a 1,000-year-old bronze axe head; presumably a family heirloom. Only the central part of the tumulus was investigated and it is entirely possible that more discoveries are waiting to be found on the outer edges. It stands today in the back gardens of two houses in Fitzwalter Road. Other finds have been made in the area and it is thought that this whole area was once an ancient cemetery.

AUGUST 10TH

2003: This was the hottest day ever recorded in Colchester, the temperature reaching 95 degrees Fahrenheit or 35 Celsius. This was only a few degrees short of the all-time national record which was reached at Gravesend on that day, when the thermometer rose a little over 100 degrees. This was a very hot August across the whole country and this is reflected in the meteorological records for Colchester. The town recorded 247 hours of sunshine that month. There was very little rain; less than a third of an inch fell in the town over August.

East Anglia is generally one of the driest places in the United Kingdom. Colchester's average annual rainfall is only 17.8 inches; a good deal less than London. This is because, being on the east side of England, the town is less exposed to weather fronts which sweep in from the Atlantic. This tends to give Colchester a more continental weather pattern, meaning the surrounding area is prone to droughts rather than heavy rainfall. This lack of rain has made the Essex coast a popular destination for holidaymakers since Victorian times.

AUGUST 11TH

1942: On this day one of the worst losses of life from enemy action in Essex during the Second World War occurred. At 1.40 in the morning, four 500lb bombs landed on Severalls Mental Hospital. One failed to explode, but the other three hit the laundry and one of the female wards, killing a total of thirty-eight patients. All were elderly, aged in the main in their sixties and seventies; all were women.

The hospital had not been the target of the German bombers – they were actually attacking military installations in the area. Incredibly, the damaged buildings were not demolished and made safe for another twenty years. Twenty-three of the women who died in this incident were buried in one grave in Colchester Cemetery. The stone above the grave bears the following inscription:

Could one of us have held your hand, or heard your last farewell?
The parting would not have been so bad, for those that mourn you still.

In 2010, a plaque was erected near this grave, telling the story of the bombing at Severalls.

AUGUST 12TH

1904: The new church of St Mary's at West Bergholt was consecrated on this day. It was the second church of this name in the village, which lies to the north of Colchester. The church of St Mary the Virgin had stood in West Bergholt since the Middle Ages. Over the years, the gradual shift of population to other districts had so reduced its congregation that by the late nineteenth century the decision was made to build another church, closer to where people were actually living.

St Mary the Virgin had a history of being unlucky with its vicars. In the sixteenth century, one did not turn up for services because he was in the pub, while just after the end of the Civil War, another was found to be in the habit of appearing drunk and swearing at the congregation during services.

When the old church was officially declared redundant in 1975, archaeological excavations were carried out at the same time as essential work to prevent the building collapsing. It was found that the church dated from much earlier than the main fabric, which was erected in the thirteenth century. It was thought that the church had begun as a small Saxon chapel which had been greatly enlarged after the Norman Conquest.

AUGUST 13TH

1866: H.G. Wells was born on this day. His connection with Colchester is an odd one. His comic novel, *The History of Mr Polly*, is usually assumed to be set in Kent. At the time that he wrote it though, Wells was living in Essex at Dunmow. He was a regular visitor to Colchester, which he mentions in another of his novels, *The War of the Worlds. The History of Mr Polly* is thought to be at least partly autobiographical; H.G. Wells worked in a clothing shop for a time, just like the novel's hero. At the time that he was writing *The History of Mr Polly* and visiting Colchester, there was a clothing shop in St Botolph's Street run by H.G. Polly. Could this have been the inspiration behind Wells' book?

There are other odd resonances between the book and Colchester. In the book, Polly fakes his suicide and torches his shop. In 1893 in Colchester, a fire took place in a tailor's shop, leading to the discovery of the badly charred body of the owner, who had apparently hanged himself before setting fire to his premises. Near to Mr Polly's shop in the book is a shop owned by a man called Clamp. Almost next to H.G. Polly's shop in St Botolph's Street was a shop run by a Mr Clamp, suggesting that it is at least possible that *The History of Mr Polly* was actually set in Colchester.

AUGUST 14TH

1902: John 'Chalky' White was born on this day. He lived the last forty-five years of his life in the village of Great Wigborough near Colchester. He was born in London and joined the Rifle Brigade when he was 17. This was the beginning of a long army career, which was to be distinguished by his remarkable ability at marksmanship: he won the King's Medal at Bisley for best shot on no fewer than three occasions.

After the end of the Second World War, John White settled in Great Wigborough. He was a member of the Territorial Army for fourteen years after the war ended. It was as a member of Colchester Rifle Club that he really made his mark in his later years and was still shooting in competitions at the age of 76; an astonishing feat. It was at this age that he achieved an almost incredible forty-nine out of fifty at 600 yards; winning the club's Admiral Hutton Cup in the process. He was still competing at Bisley when he was in his eighties. He died at Welshwood Nursing Home in Colchester in October 1992, at the age of 90; perhaps one of the best British rifle shots of the twentieth century.

AUGUST 15TH

1924: Dr William Augustus Maybury died on this day. His memorial is a curious one, consisting of a brick-built grotto with seats in Castle Park. It is a very modest little grotto, with no roof; merely three short walls and a few benches.

Dr Maybury, who lived in West Stockwell Street in Colchester, practiced medicine in Colchester from 1875 until his death almost fifty years later. His son, Horace, also became a doctor who moved to London. We know that his grandson was called Horace Claude Maybury and that he served in the Royal Flying Corps during the First World War. Beyond this, we know nothing really of this once popular doctor.

Colchester has more odd little memorials to its once important residents than other towns. One stumbles across them everywhere; drinking fountains, plaques, cattle troughs and many other marks of the passing of the once famous, at least locally. We will never know who thought of or paid for the little grotto in Castle Park. The last record of Dr Maybury is a notice in the *London Gazette* on March 30th 1926, urging any outstanding creditors to come forward before the late doctor's executors wound up his affairs.

AUGUST 16TH

1907: A boy swimming in the River Alde at Rendham in Suffolk made a strange discovery on this day. It was the life-size, bronze head of the emperor Claudius and it showed signs of having been hacked off from a statue, rather than being a bust. The tilt of the head strongly suggests that this was an equestrian statue. Where did it come from and how did it come to be found in a river in Suffolk? We can never answer these questions with complete assurance, but it is certainly possible to hazard a guess.

We know that after his death, Claudius was made a god and that a temple dedicated to him stood in Colchester; its remains lie beneath the castle. The temple was sacked and burned during the Boudican revolt of AD 60 and it is reasonable to suppose that booty was carried away from the ruin of the Roman city. The Celts were enthusiastic head hunters and decapitated skulls from this period have turned up in many rivers and streams, where they were probably deposited as votive offerings to the local gods. The most likely explanation was that the statue of Claudius was thrown down and mutilated during the destruction of Colchester; we saw similar treatment meted out to a statue of Saddam Hussein after the fall of Baghdad. The head could then have been carried into the territory of the Iceni and cast as a votive offering into the river.

AUGUST 17TH

1739: On this day, the Assizes ended at Chelmsford. George Grey, a plumber and glazier, and another man who was a barber, both of Colchester, were convicted of 'Sodomical Practices'. They were lucky, the penalty for their activities amounted only to a spell in the pillory and a short term of imprisonment – a few years earlier and they could easily have faced the death penalty.

How very different is the situation in Colchester today. For example, Colchester offers the Pride Wine Bar, an exclusively gay bar, Vallies Lounge Bar and Club, and the Enigma Skyrooms, which offers 'theme nights and an amazing atmosphere'. In addition to places such as these, there is also The Outhouse, which offers a range of services for gay people, from counselling and advice about homophobia to work with young people and information about sexual health. Things certainly have come a long way since poor George Grey and his friend ended up in the pillory.

AUGUST 18TH

330: St Helena, mother of the Roman Emperor Constantine I, died on this day. In the Catholic Church, August 18th is her feast day, although the Anglicans prefer May 21st. Very ancient traditions associate Helena with Colchester; of which city she is the patron saint. Geoffrey of Monmouth, for instance, suggests that she was the daughter of King Cole of Colchester; the same King Cole who features in the popular nursery rhyme. What is certain is the connection of her son with Britain; he was declared emperor in York.

Helena was a devout Christian and when her son became emperor, she made a pilgrimage to the Holy Land to search for the remains of Jesus' cross. According to some accounts, she found both the cross and the nails used to fix Christ to it. It is a fact that the crest of Colchester makes extensive reference to Helena's pilgrimage and the relics which she uncovered during it. The shield is red, symbolising the blood of Christ; there are three crowns, representing the crowns of the three kings who came to do homage to baby Jesus, and there is also a green cross; the living cross which Helena found. Finally, beneath each crown is a large nail, which are the nails which Helena found and brought back from the Holy Land.

AUGUST 19TH

1874: Henry Wolton died on this day at the age of 71. It is sometimes assumed that Colchester's Oyster Feast is an ancient tradition, but we really have Henry Wolton Esq. JP to thank for it.

In the years just before Queen Victoria came to the throne, there was a lot of concern about corrupt election practices and ratepayers' money being squandered by local authorities. The two things often went hand-in-hand, with corporations inviting people whose support they required to lavish dinners, where they were wooed. In Colchester, the annual Election Dinner, when the new town council was chosen, was a typical example of the sort of thing which some were uneasy about. Dickens lampooned events like these in *The Pickwick Papers*.

In 1835, there was reform of local government, which forbade civic feasting of this sort. When Henry Wolton was made Mayor in 1845, he got round these restrictions by holding a Corporation Lunch at his own expense, to which he invited 200 guests. This evolved into the Oyster Feast and was immensely popular – so popular, in fact, that Wolton was elected Mayor six times in later years.

August 20th

1987: This is the day that *Continuity and Change, Volume 2* by Peter King was published. King has written extensively about newspaper reporting and how it influenced the perception of crime and disorder in eighteenth-century England. In *Continuity and Change*, he examines what is sometimes called 'The Great Colchester Crime Wave' – a period of several months in 1765 when it appeared that Colchester had been gripped by an unprecedented spate of robberies, assaults and murders.

In both *Continuity and Change* and other works, King explores the idea that the rapid growth in newspaper circulation towards the end of the eighteenth century created competition between them to see who could provide the most lurid accounts of crime and executions. Even the *London Times* was not immune to this temptation. In East Anglia, there was a furious circulation war between the *Ipswich Journal* and a number of newer weekly papers. The ones with the most startling headlines tended to sell more copies and so the proprietors began to give prominence to robberies and murders in order to boost sales. Glancing through local newspapers from Essex and Suffolk from that time suggests that the average citizen of Colchester was not safe in his own bed at night and that the streets were infested with footpads, rapists and killers. Such tactics might ring a bell for modern journalists!

AUGUST 21ST

2011: This is the day that the Revd Jo Dudley conducted her last service at St Luke's Church in Tiptree. Since the ordination of female priests was permitted by the Church of England in the early 1990s, more and more of the vicars whom one encounters are women. Without them, the Anglican Church would be hard-pressed to keep going.

Jo Dudley is a local woman, whose family live a stone's throw from Tiptree. She has ancestors from the nineteenth century buried in the churchyard at great Braxted. It is worth mentioning that the Revd Dudley also had responsibility for All Saints' Church at Great Braxted. Jo Dudley's leaving of her parish was conducted in a quintessentially English fashion. A few weeks before she was due to go, the Tiptree Handbell team were hosting an evening which would be something of a farewell event for the Revd Dudley. She left a fortnight later, with no more ado.

AUGUST 22ND

1642: The home of Sir John Lucas, a wealthy landowner near Colchester, was looted by an anti-Royalist mob on this day. Despite the fact that Colchester was held by Royalist forces for two months during the English Civil War, the general mood of this part of Essex had always been a little unenthusiastic about High Church practices and submitting to noble landlords.

Sir Lucas and his brothers, Thomas and Charles, had been knighted by Charles I. In 1638, with rebellion brewing in both England and Ireland, Sir Thomas was given an army command in Ireland. He helped to put down uprisings in that country, before returning to England and serving the King on the Royalist side in the civil war. Meanwhile, his brother John was preparing for the outbreak of war in England. When the King raised his standard at Nottingham and summoned his supporters to join him, Sir John Lucas began assembling horses and arms to take to the King's service. This enraged the ordinary citizens of Colchester, who descended on Lucas' house as a mob and prevented him from taking help to the King. For good measure, they then surged into his mansion and looted whatever took their fancy.

AUGUST 23RD

1993: The Tiptree-based firm JobServe was registered at Companies House on this day. JobServe was the world's first internet recruitment service. It was started by Robbie Cowling and John Witney, and from the very beginning had its headquarters at Tiptree in Essex, although their registered office is in Colchester.

When JobServe was launched, the World Wide Web was not yet available for public access. It was a far-sighted gamble to start a business based entirely in cyberspace, but it was a gamble which paid off handsomely. In May 1994, JobServe achieved another first with a 'jobs by email' service. Later that year, they established a presence on the recently devised web.

Since those early days, JobServe has gone from strength to strength. It now has main offices in Cleveland and Atlanta in the USA, Sydney in Australia, Ottawa in Canada and Bangkok in Thailand. Their site receives over one and a half million visits a month, which result in a million applications for jobs. The company employs 250 staff. Robbie Cowling is now a millionaire many times over, being worth an estimated £105 million. He is also the owner of Colchester United Football Club.

August 24th

1937: This is the day that the *London Gazette* published the application of Walter Lloyd of 118 North Station Road, Colchester to change his name by Deed Poll. The name which Mr Lloyd wished to adopt? None other than that of Leon Petulengro. Thus one of the contenders for the title of 'King of the Gypsies' made his appearance in the world of professional Romanies.

There is some doubt about the name of Walter Lloyd's father. He was variously known as Walter Lloyd himself, but also as Smith and, in later years, the stupendously romantic Xavier Petulengro. It was this which prompted his son to change his name. In the same year that he changed his name to Petulengro, the erstwhile Walter Lloyd married another Colchester resident; Illeana Smith.

Leon Petulengro, as he became universally known, was tremendously popular as an astrologer, and wrote a number of books on the topic, all of which traded heavily on his supposed Romany background. At the very least, it is fair to say that a book on fortune-telling by plain Walter Lloyd might well have sold fewer copies than one by Leon Petulengro; son of the King of the Gypsies!

AUGUST 25TH

79: Pliny the Elder died on this day during the destruction of Pompei by the volcano Vesuvius. Pliny was an industrious writer who churned out reams of material. His final, and most famous, work was *Naturalis Historia* or *Natural History*. This is really the world's first encyclopaedia and its layout has been followed by almost all subsequent works of this sort.

The *Naturalis Historia* covers almost every field of human knowledge, ranging from botany and zoology to astronomy, geology and the history of art. It is of interest to us because this is the first written reference to any town in Britain. Pliny talks of Camulodunum; which later became Colchester. This is solid evidence for the claim that Colchester is Britain's oldest town.

When Claudius invaded Britain in AD 43, his army apparently made a beeline for Colchester; it being regarded as the main town in the country. Indeed, for twenty years or so, until its destruction by Boudicca's army in AD 60, Colchester was the official capital of the province of Britannia. Little wonder then that such an important place should have found its way into an encyclopaedia being compiled at that time.

AUGUST 26TH

1978: On this day, ancient wooden piles were uncovered beneath the causeway linking Mersea Island with the mainland. The causeway, known as the Strood, is the only road leading to Mersea. Because of the Roman remains on the island, the suspicion had always been that the earliest roadway would have dated from this time. In 1978, a water pipe was being laid from the mainland to Mersea and the chance was taken to investigate the early history of the Strood.

When stout oak stakes were found during digging, there was great excitement. To begin with, the assumption was that these must surely date back to the Roman occupation. However, carbon dating showed clearly that these timbers were in fact from no earlier than AD 530; a century after the Romans left Britain. The final date fixed upon was that the causeway had first been constructed between AD 684 and AD 702.

There were two reasons for archaeologists to be excited about the results of the excavation of the Strood. The first and most obvious was that this was the first Saxon causeway from this period ever examined. The second reason had a wider application. Dendrochronology dates wood far more accurately than carbon dating, by measuring and comparing tree rings. These are then compared with samples of known age. The sequence used in this country until 1978 did not stretch back beyond AD 682. The material from the Strood therefore enabled archaeologists to track the sequence back as far as AD 480, when the Strood timbers had begun to grow.

AUGUST 27TH

1864: A drinking fountain near North Gate in Colchester – presented to the people of Colchester by their MP, Taverner John Miller – was unveiled on this day by Mayor J. Bishop.

Taverner John Miller ran a whaling operation from, of all unlikely places, the area around the Victoria Tower gardens near the Houses of Parliament. By his late forties though, he had decided to go into politics. He was first elected MP of Maldon, but allegations of corruption led to the result being set aside. In February 1857, he stood for Colchester at a by election. He did not win, but the next month there was a General Election and this time he made it into Parliament as the Conservative member for the town. He was to hold the seat for the next ten years until his sudden and unexpected resignation on February 5th 1867. He took the post of Steward of the Manor of Northstead on leaving the Commons and the following month the reason for his abrupt leaving of the Commons became clear. He had in fact been ill for some time and died on March 27th 1867.

AUGUST 28TH

1648: During the English Civil War, the town of Colchester was for a time held by the Royalists. It was besieged by a Parliamentary army commanded by Lord-General Fairfax. When the town finally surrendered, the ordinary soldiers were all pardoned. The decision was taken to make an example of the aristocratic leaders of the Royalists and four of them were tried by court-martial and sentenced to death; the executions to be carried out by firing squad. Those condemned were Sir Charles Lucas, Sir George Lisle, Sir Bernard Gascoigne and Colonel Farre.

Gascoigne was discovered to be an Italian citizen and was spared. Farre escaped, which left only Lucas and Lisle to face the firing squad. The executions were carried out in the evening. Both men went bravely to their deaths and a monument in the grounds of Colchester Castle now marks the site of the execution. Almost as soon as they had died, the two men were treated as martyrs to the Royalist cause. Fifty years after their deaths, it was said that no grass would grow where their blood had been shed.

AUGUST 29TH

2011: According to a report in the *Daily Gazette* on this day, a couple became stranded on the Strood, the causeway which leads to Mersea Island. Mersea is the easternmost inhabited island in the British Isles and it is sometimes easy to forget that it is actually an island. For most of the time, the road leading to Mersea looks like any other. The only thing is, it does tend to flood at high tide. Despite warning signs, some people will always take a chance on being able to get across before the water rises. In 1954, a driver who took this gamble was drowned when he inadvertently drove off the Strood while crossing it at high tide.

The couple in the more recent news report started driving across at high tide and then stopped when their vehicle began filling with water. They dialled 999 and, as a result, the Mersea lifeboat was launched and two fire engines were despatched to the scene. The situation was not, however, too serious, because by the time the emergency services had arrived, the couple had left their car and walked along the Strood to the shore.

AUGUST 30TH

1885: Thomas Thornycroft, the sculptor, died on this day. The son of a Cheshire farmer, Thornycroft moved to London when young and trained as an artist. His larger-than-life-size statue of Queen Victoria was much admired at the Great Exhibition in 1851; not least by the Queen herself. His connection with Colchester is indirect although strong. If the town of Colchester has a *bete noire*, it must surely be the Queen of the Iceni who swept south in AD 60 and burned Colchester to the ground, killing everybody upon whom she and her army could lay their hands. We do not really know what Boudicca looked like and yet we all have a vivid mental image whenever we hear her name. She is stately and tall, her arm raised imperiously and she is riding in a chariot with blades attached to the wheels. Whether or not this image has any historical veracity, it is what springs at once to most minds when they hear the name 'Boudicca'.

We have Thomas Thornycroft to thank for our definitive idea of the Queen of the Britons. Flushed with the success of his statue of Victoria, he embarked in later years upon a massive and monumental statue of Boudicca. This masterpiece was not actually cast in bronze until 1902; seventeen years after Thornycroft's death. Today, it stands at the end of Westminster Bridge; an archetypal image of ancient Britain.

August 31st

1549: Six men were hanged in Colchester on this day for rebellion. 1549 was an uneasy year. Henry VIII was dead and some people felt that it was time for some radical changes in the country. In early July, the so-called Kett's Rebellion broke out in Norfolk. Some peasants began tearing down the fences of wealthy landowners, one of whom did not oppose them, but proposed himself as their leader. Robert Kett was a landowner near Norwich and he eventually led a crowd of over 16,000 discontented agricultural workers in an assault on Norwich, which was at that time England's second largest city. Amazingly, on July 22nd 1549, his ragtag army managed to seize the city.

In Colchester, a priest from Norfolk spread news of the revolt and capture of Norwich and a number of men thought that they might be able to start something of the sort in their own town. Two men were convicted of treason, but subsequently pardoned.

After Kett's rebellion was put down by the army, some of those who had taken part fled to Colchester and began to try and foment sedition there. After a trial in front of Thomas Darcy and the Earl of Oxford, six men were sentenced to death and hanged; three in front of the city gates and three outside the castle. This marked the end of any thoughts of rebellion in the Colchester area.

September 1st

1999: The British army's largest brigade was formed on this day. 16 Air Assault Brigade is the most recently formed brigade in the British Army and it is based in Colchester. It was formed by the amalgamation of 24 Airmobile and 5 Airborne Brigades and it was described on its formation as the most powerful airborne force this country has ever deployed.

16 Air Assault Brigade consists of 6,000 men and women who can be sent rapidly to anywhere in the world. It is a vital part of the Joint Helicopter Command, which was formed the following month in order to bring the helicopters of all three services under a single command structure. The Brigade has played some key roles in world affairs since its formation. In 2001, for example, it was instrumental in helping to establish the UN's International Security Assistance Force in Afghanistan.

A combined army and RAF headquarters in Colchester coordinates the activities of 16 Air Assault Brigade, which contains elements from a number of units such as the Parachute Regiment and the Army Air Corps. Alongside artillery units and the Royal Engineers, the brigade is a world-class fighting force.

SEPTEMBER 2ND

1939: On this day, thousands of children evacuated from London arrived in Colchester. Since the Munich Conference of 1938, plans had been made that in the event of war with Germany, children would be taken from Britain's big cities and dispersed into the countryside. It was widely expected that bombing raids in the opening days would render life in the cities unendurable.

Because Colchester was on the main line from Liverpool Street to the Essex coast, it was an obvious place to send children, so that they could then be forwarded, as it were, to the smaller villages. When German troops marched into Poland on September 1st 1939, it was clear that war could not be averted. Over the next three days, 14,000 children from London arrived in Colchester. Many came without their parents; accompanied only by school teachers and welfare workers. In addition to the thousands of children, there were a large number of mothers and babies as well.

Three Colchester schools, namely Wilson Marriage, St John's Green and Canterbury Road, were employed as reception centres where the children were tended to before being despatched to their final destinations. Within a week, 5,500 had been sent to Lexden, the same number to Tendring district and the rest to Brightlingsea, Wivenhoe and West Mersea.

SEPTEMBER 3RD

1995: Ivor Crewe was appointed Vice Chancellor of the University of Essex on this day. Sir Ivor Martin Crewe, as he has been since 2006, was born on December 15th 1945. He was educated at Manchester Grammar School and Oxford University. He had a career in political journalism before being appointed to the post at the University of Essex. He moved to Colchester in 1971 and so really counted by that time as a local.

Sir Ivor remained Vice Chancellor until 2007. In 2003, he was made High Steward of Colchester, an honorary position which he held until 2009. He was the twenty-second High Steward of Colchester.

The post of High Steward of Colchester was created by Royal Charter in 1635, although all powers associated with it were removed in 1835. The role is today restricted to representing the town at Remembrance Day and similar purely ceremonial functions. No expenses are paid for any duties undertaken by the holder of the post. Sir Ivor asked to be relieved of the role in 2009, after being appointed Master of University College Oxford. He felt that it would be unfair to the town to have a High Steward who was not even living in the town. The second High Steward of Colchester though, the Duke of Albermerle, did not even set foot in the town throughout the whole course of his life!

September 4th

2009: The *Essex County Standard* reported on this day that, according to government estimates, Colchester was the largest borough in the county. With a population of around 180,000, it is the second most populous non-London borough, coming just behind Northampton.

The borough of Colchester covers 125 square miles, stretching from the Vale of Dedham on the Suffolk border to Mersea Island on the North Sea in the south. The largest town is Colchester, but there are a number of other towns in the borough, including Tiptree, which, although technically a village, is a town in all other senses. Over 92 per cent of the population are white and the life expectancy of females at birth is 83, compared to 79 for males.

A very high percentage identify themselves as Christian – over 70 per cent. Fewer than 1 per cent were Muslim and even fewer described themselves as Jewish. Although about 8 per cent of those living in the Borough of Colchester belong to an ethnic minority, there is no single large group: 1.1 per cent are Indian, 0.9 per cent African, 0.4 per cent Caribbean and 0.3 per cent Bangladeshi.

September 5th

1746: John Skinner was hanged at Chelmsford on this day. Skinner was one of the most famous smugglers in the Colchester area and his trade was an open secret to those who knew him. He was generally known as either 'Colchester Jack' or 'Saucy Jack', the latter because of the amount of time and money he spent in brothels.

John Skinner was famous for his ferocious temper, which was, in the end, the death of him. He quarrelled with Daniel Brett, his servant, and shot him. Brett died of his wound and Skinner found himself under arrest and charged with murder. The trial at Chelmsford was by way of being a formality; there was no doubt at all as to what had happened. Skinner was sentenced to death; the date of the execution fixed for September 5th.

The night before he was due to be hanged, Skinner somehow managed to get hold of a knife. It was a very small one, but he nevertheless stabbed himself repeatedly with it in an attempt to cheat the gallows of its prey. He failed to sever any major blood vessels though and was still alive the next morning. He was so weak from his wounds, that he was unable to speak and so died without making the traditional speech from the scaffold.

September 6th

1996: On this day a report in *The Times* tells of the finding of a board game in a 2,000-year-old grave at Stanway, near Colchester. The grave, dating from the first few years following the Roman invasion of AD 43, contained a variety of strange objects, suggesting that the individual interred here was of very high status.

Of the person whose grave this was, there were no identifiable remains at all – only a jar full of cremated bone; not enough to tell us whether this was even a man or woman. In addition to the board game, surgical tools were found, as well as a set of mysterious metal rods of unknown purpose. There was also something very like a tea strainer, which container traces of the herb mugwort. Together, these items suggested somebody like a doctor or healer. As a result, the grave's occupant became known as 'The Druid of Colchester'.

The playing board, which has become known as The Stanway Game, was 21 by 15 inches in size and divided into squares like a chessboard. It was accompanied by twenty-six blue and white glass playing pieces. How the game was played is a complete mystery. The best guess is that it was a game of strategy, something like draughts. There is some doubt as to whether it is even a game. One suggestion made was that, combined with the metal rods mentioned above, the whole thing might have been some means for divining the future!

SEPTEMBER 7TH

1965: On this day, the Norman Way School opened as one of the new comprehensive schools meant to replace the Secondary Modern Schools in which the majority of Colchester's children had previously been educated. It was located for the first two years of its existence in the Greyfriars area of Colchester. During this time, the main buildings were being constructed in Prettygate. For the next twenty years, there was pretty much continuous building and expansion of the school. There are still plans to expand the school even further. In 2009, the school applied for permission to extend Norman Way into the neighbouring fields and so allow it to take on pupils from two other schools. At the time of writing, this plan is currently on hold. When the Norman Way School was built, it was intended that Norman Way itself would become an inner ring road for Colchester, but it was later felt that having to make their way across a main road regularly would put the pupils at hazard and the scheme was abandoned.

In 1993, shortly after it had become a technology college, Norman Way School changed its name to the Philip Morant College.

September 8th

1971: Tiptree Heath was registered as a Site of Special Scientific Interest on this day. The sandy gravel formation upon which Tiptree and its heath stands was formed over 350,000 years ago, during a glacial period. It has been recognised as common land since 1401.

Today, Tiptree Heath has been reduced to an area of sixty acres. At one time, heathland stretched across almost the whole of Essex which was not covered in forest. These few acres are all that remains. Tiptree Heath is the only place in Essex where you can find all three native species of heather growing together: Common Ling, Bell Heather and Cross-Leaved Heath all coexist happily; each exploiting slightly different parts of the ecosystem. This is also the only place in Essex where you can find allseed and chaffweed plants growing wild.

The heath is not only home to unusual plants. Among the less common animals likely to be found here are water voles and dormice, while there is also a resident population of badgers and grass snakes. Tiptree Heath is jointly managed by the Essex Wildlife Trust and the Friends of Tiptree Heath.

SEPTEMBER 9TH

1859: The *Essex and Suffolk Gazette* carried an interesting piece on this day which threw light on the process for obtaining licences to serve spirits in public houses. At that time, there was not the sharp division which there is today between off-licences and pubs. One could run a beer shop, but still not be allowed to serve spirits. The whole question of drinking and drunkenness was a very keenly debated one in Colchester, partly because of the presence of so many soldiers who wanted places to drink, but also because some in the town felt that having a large number of pubs lowered the tone of the area.

The British Grenadier was at 67 Military Road and they applied to the Justices for a licence to serve spirits. The application was vigorously contested by solicitors acting for other publicans in the area. The magistrates themselves were a little concerned that in this street there seemed to be nothing but pubs, to which the soldiers not unnaturally flocked. The application was turned down on the grounds that there were already enough licensed premises in the area. The next year, the owner of The British Grenadier was back, this time with a memorial signed by a clergyman, stating that Mr Neville, who ran the beer shop, was a respectable person. It was enough to sway the Justices and they granted the licence.

SEPTEMBER 10TH

1791: Sarah Wallis was born in Colchester on this day. She became famous in the early nineteenth century under her married name, Lee. When she was 22, Sara married Edward Bowdich. The couple had a daughter and then her husband took a job in West Africa, leaving his family behind in England. Mrs Lee then, entirely of her own accord, followed her husband to Africa. While there, she became something of an expert on the local wildlife. By the time they returned to this country, Sara Lee had another two children.

When her husband died in 1824, the young widow needed a way of supporting herself and she turned to writing to do so. She had barely begun her writing career when she remarried, this time Robert Lee; it is as Sara Lee that she published her most well-known works. These range from school books such as *Elements of Natural History* to academic works like *British Birds* and *Taxidermy*.

Writing scientific works of this sort at that time was an exceedingly unusual thing for a woman to do. Nevertheless, Mrs Lee was acknowledged by many famous men of the day to be a leading expert in the field of natural history. She died in 1856.

September 11th

1822: On this day one of the largest sums of money ever stolen in nineteenth-century England disappeared in Colchester. A representative of a bank at Ipswich was returning from London with a parcel containing £31,199 in untraceable bank notes. He shared a stagecoach with three men who were also travelling from London, and placed the money in the locker for parcels. At Colchester he left the stagecoach for a short time and on his return he found the three missing. With them had gone the £31,199.

At a time when a working man might earn £50 a year, the present-day value of this amount is incalculable. It would certainly be the equivalent to millions. The bank offered a reward of £5,000 for the return of the money, but a month later nothing had been discovered. In fact, the theft seems to have been part of an elaborate scam on the part of those who took the money. They must surely have known that details of the notes would be circulated and that the chances of passing over £30,000 in high denomination notes was negligible. Even £5 and £10 notes were great rarities in those days. In the event, they engaged solicitors to negotiate with the bank. They received a small reward – which the bank refused to reveal – for returning the notes, almost all of which were eventually recovered. The men responsible for this audacious piece of work were never found.

SEPTEMBER 12TH

2007: Professor Jules Pretty found the shrivelled corpse of a strange, small animal on this day while walking along the shore on Mersea Island. He was wise enough to photograph the thing and send the picture to Dougal Urquhart, a keen naturalist who runs a blog on Mersea's natural history. The odd-looking creature was identified as a mink; the first ever to be recorded on Mersea.

Mink were imported into this country from the USA from 1929 onwards. They were farmed for their fur, but a large number escaped and now live wild across England, Scotland and Wales. They are very similar to and belong to the same family as weasels and stoats. They live a semi-aquatic life, being generally found near rivers and ponds, where they feed on fish; being particularly fond of eels. They will also eat rabbits, birds and anything else they can get hold of.

Mink are found throughout Essex and have been recorded on the mainland shore near to Mersea. It is supposed that the bare expanse of the Strood – the causeway linking Mersea to the mainland – might prove unattractive to these ferocious predators. The specimen found by Professor Pretty looked as though it probably drowned in the sea and there have been no further reports of mink on Mersea Island.

SEPTEMBER 13TH

2010: The old East Anglian tradition of smuggling goods such as tobacco past the excise men was, according to a report in the Colchester edition of the *Gazette* on this day, alive and well in the area. Still, it's an ill wind which blows nobody any good and in this particular case there were definite beneficiaries of the smugglers. These were various reptiles at Colchester Zoo.

The plot was a brilliant one. Ten million cigarettes were to be imported at Felixstowe in Suffolk, cunningly concealed beneath crates of tomatoes. Unfortunately, the customs officers were wise to old tricks of this sort and the cigarettes were confiscated. Had they got through, it would have cheated the Inland Revenue out of about £2 million in unpaid duty. Which left the problem of what to do with the tomatoes. Fortunately, somebody thought of Colchester Zoo and the entire consignment was sent there. The rare tortoises and iguanas apparently relished the unexpected addition to their diet.

SEPTEMBER 14TH

1820: The Essex and Colchester Hospital opened in Lexden Road on this day. Plans for an infirmary for poor people were drawn up in 1818 and land on the south side of Lexden Road was bought. We sometimes forget that even before the establishment of the National Health Service in 1948, extensive provision was being made for those who could not afford medical treatment. Throughout the nineteenth century, the Essex and Colchester Hospital survived through a combination of vigorous fundraising and regular charitable events such a bazaars.

In 1920, financial difficulties meant that the hospital was forced to begin charging in-patients £1 a week for their keep. This only represented a fraction though of the true cost, which was still made up primarily of charitable donations from the well-off. The hospital was run by a management committee which included the Lord Lieutenant of Essex, the Mayor of Colchester and local MPs, all of whom subscribed regular annual amounts for the upkeep of the hospital. In 1948, the Essex and Colchester Hospital was taken over by the newly formed NHS and from that time on, patients did not have to pay towards treatment.

September 15th

1372: On this day, Colchester's first borough council was elected. As Colchester grew, it was clear that some sort of local authority needed to be exercised. Although the King in London was the ultimate ruler and the Church also had a say in day-to-day life, some kind of accountable body was necessary to maintain order in the town.

The methods used to select those who would serve on the new council showed the first stirrings of the democratic process in this country. Although elections as we now know them were unknown, it was nevertheless clearly felt that the officers should have the backing of the people and that without this, their actions would lack legitimacy. The process was begun by choosing four men to represent each of the town's wards. These men were to be selected 'by the advice of the whole commonalty'. They in turn each found five men to sit on the council. These were to be sixteen of the wisest and wealthiest men in the town.

Although this method of putting together a local council leaves much to be desired and is plainly open to corruption, it was a great improvement on the previous situation, where ordinary people had no say at all in who was to govern them.

SEPTEMBER 16TH

1428: Father Abraham, a preacher from Colchester who rejected the Catholic Church, was burned at the stake on this day. He was one of a group of renegade priests who had become disillusioned with traditional Christianity and wished to reform it so that it was more in keeping with the Gospel. This was a dangerous enterprise in early fifteenth-century England and the priests could not really have been surprised at the fate which later befell them.

Father Abraham and John Waddon were both leaders of this movement in East Anglia. Both were from Colchester. Among their declared beliefs were that the Pope was the Antichrist, that prayers made in every place are equally acceptable to God, that one ought not to go on pilgrimages, that holy water is no different from water drawn from a well, and that nobody should pray to saints.

Today, none of this is particularly controversial, but it was hot stuff indeed in 1428 and the greatest efforts were made to catch the men who were leading the people astray from their proper allegiance to the Church. All those arrested from this group were subsequently burned; some in Essex and the others in Norfolk.

September 17th

1557: On this day, two women were burnt at the stake in the grounds of Colchester Castle. When Henry VIII's daughter Mary came to the throne in 1553, she tried to reverse the English Reformation initiated by her father and restore the Roman Catholic faith to supremacy in this country. The means by which she tried to do so were simple and brutal; those who did not accept Catholicism were treated as heretics and liable to be burned alive.

Essex in general and Colchester in particular were well known for their adherence to Protestantism and this was especially so with some women. In August 1557, a group of men and women were burned in Colchester. Agnes Bongeor was scheduled to burn at the same time, but the warrant for her execution mis-spelt her name and so she remained in her cell at Colchester Castle. Another woman, Margaret Thurston, had been arrested for heresy but, afraid of being burned, had recanted and agreed to rejoin the Catholic Church. She later changed her mind and once again rejected Catholicism. She was returned to prison and on the morning of September 17th, she and Agnes Bongeor were taken out and tied to stakes near the castle. They were then burned alive.

September 18th

1543: John Lucas was appointed Town Clerk of Colchester on this day. He had been born in Suffolk in 1512 and then practiced as a barrister in London. His father was already a lawyer and it was to this that he owed his legal career.

John Lucas' rise was meteoric. In 1537, at the age of 25, he was appointed to the Essex bench and shortly afterwards married a woman from that county and settled in Colchester. His success owed as much to his political instincts as any natural talent. In 1539, for instance, he was one of three prosecuting counsel at the trial of the Abbot of Colchester. This was quite a good position to be in at the height of the English Reformation. A year later, he had been appointed Steward to the Earl of Oxford, whose family at that time owned Colchester Castle.

The patronage of the Earl of Oxford was enough to secure Lucas both the position of Town Clerk of Colchester and also allow him to become its MP. His fortunes changed dramatically with the accession of Queen Mary. Lucas had been one of those who had supported Lady Jane Grey's brief elevation to Queen and Mary never forgave him. He spent a short time in prison, an experience which left its mark upon him. He died in 1556.

September 19th

2009: Those fortunate enough to have been in the vicinity of the Magdalen Hall in Colchester's Wimpole Road on this day would have had the opportunity to have coffee with Bob Russell, the town's MP. The Liberal Democrat website which enticed people with this opportunity also carries a great deal of information about Mr Russell. The various snippets include the following fact: 'A further claim to fame — Bob Russell could be the fastest typing MP (seventy-five words per minute)! The phrase 'could be' rather takes the edge of this claim. Has any research been done about the typing speeds of MPs?

SEPTEMBER 20TH

1937: This is the day that the new vicar at St Andrew's Church in Langenhoe first encountered the supernatural activity which led to his church being described as 'the most haunted church in England'. Reverend Ernest Merryweather arrived at his new parish in 1937. Langenhoe is a small village just south of Colchester and he expected a peaceful stay. He recorded in his journal that he was alone in the church and that the day was still. Suddenly and without warning, the great west door of the church crashed shut.

From then on it was one thing after another: thumping noises from the belfry, flowers on the altar removed and scattered on the pews, strange smells and the shade of a veiled lady who appeared from nowhere. It was all most disturbing. The manifestations eased up during the war years (1939-1945), but as soon as peace returned, so did the ghosts. Perhaps surprisingly, Revd Merryweather stayed at St Andrew's for over fifteen years.

The fabric of the building had been badly damaged in the 1884 earthquake and it was abandoned as being unsafe in 1955; finally being demolished seven years later.

September 21st

1660: A new law came into force on this day for the better regulation of the making of bays. Since the weavers in Colchester's Dutch Quarter had been making bays (baize) there quite well for centuries, it is interesting to ask why the government should suddenly have been so concerned that they passed a law specifically about this industry. The statute named Colchester as a centre for the trade and went into great detail about the making and transport of the bays being produced there.

To understand what prompted the government to introduce draconian legislation concerning the weavers and their products, it is necessary to realise that during the time of Charles II's reign, he and his government were always short of money. Earlier in 1660, an Act of Parliament had been passed for 'the speedy raising of seventy thousands pounds for the present supply of His Majesty'. As in our own time, when governments run short of ready cash, they often look around for things to tax and this is what happened with bays: all cloth made in Colchester would attract new duties when it was taken from the town and all bays would have to carry the seal of Colchester Corporation. Forging this seal could result in the death penalty. New powers were granted to the authorities to search traffic leaving Colchester to make sure that all taxes on bays were being paid.

SEPTEMBER 22ND

2011: On this day, the MYA (Make Yourself Amazing) cosmetic surgery company posted a comment by Bob Russell, MP for Colchester, on their website, which gave the impression that he was endorsing the services which they offered. He was of course doing nothing of the sort and it was in reality nothing more than another illustration of the Law of Unintended Consequences.

A short while before MYA quoted Bob Russell, he had noted approvingly that a hospital in his constituency had been put on a Department of Health sponsored list of places where cosmetic surgery was carried out by licensed practitioners. Spotting a passing bandwagon, the popular MP couldn't resist jumping aboard and while praising a local hospital, he casually mentioned the dangers of such procedures being carried out by rogue practitioners. Reporting this, the MYA site said that, 'Bob Russell MP has spoken out to urge his constituents and other potential patients to make sure that their treatment is carried out by a registered practitioner, such as those at MYA'. This gave the distinct impression that Bob Russell had recommended MYA by name to those wanting Botox. A brilliant piece of work by MYA, if a tad misleading.

SEPTEMBER 23RD

1916: This is the day that a Zeppelin was brought down near Colchester. The first blitz on London by German bombers was carried out during the First World War by giant airships called Zeppelins. On the night of September 23rd, one such Zeppelin, the L33, bombed the East End of London and then headed home. Its route took it through Essex and over Chelmsford and Colchester. Above Chelmsford, it was intercepted by a British fighter, whose pilot fired an entire drum from his machine gun into the huge, unwieldy craft. Although the hydrogen-filled airship did not catch fire, the bullet holes caused gas to leave the ruptured hull at such a rate that the Zeppelin began to lose height at the rate of 800 feet a minute.

The airship eventually crashed to earth near the village of Little Wigborough, a few miles south of Colchester. The captain and his twenty-two crew members decided to seize a boat and return to Germany across the North Sea. They were by this time surrounded by a crowd of curious villagers, one of whom the Captain asked, 'Can you tell me how far we are from Colchester?' Unfortunately, this turned out to be the local policeman, who replied phlegmatically, 'Never mind about Colchester; you come along with me.' A single, unarmed police officer thus took into custody twenty-three German airmen.

September 24th

2009: An article in the *Essex Gazette* drew attention on this day to the possibility of large, new housing developments in the village of Tiptree. Fear was expressed by local residents that this would change the nature of their village irrevocably and transform it into a town. Some writing in to the newspaper pointed out that Tiptree's population had, over the last century, risen from fewer than a thousand to the present figure of over 11,000.

Tiptree is, by some accounts, the largest village in England. The only problem with this claim is that there exists no universally accepted definition of what constitutes a village. Some would dispute that a settlement of over 11,000 people could properly be called a village. In November 1999, the parish council organised a referendum to see what residents' views were on the possibility of Tiptree's status changing from village to town. An overwhelming 88 per cent were against the proposal. For those living there, it is evidently very important that Tiptree continues to be called a village. The opposition to new housing was perhaps based upon this psychological point, rather than any objective fears that more houses would alter in any perceptible way the place itself.

SEPTEMBER 25TH

2011: The Firstsite art gallery opened in Colchester on this day. Perhaps describing the building as an 'art gallery' is too simplistic. On their website, Firstsite call themselves a 'visual arts organisation'. Their mission is evidently 'to make contemporary art relevant and life-changing for everybody'. An ambitious aim indeed!

The gallery is in what some call Colchester's 'Cultural Quarter'; that is to say near the castle and other museums in the city. On its opening, the Firstsite gallery was criticised by the *Guardian* for the physical design of the place, with its oddly sloping walls, and by the *Daily Telegraph* for the amount of money spent on the project. Ironically, despite being dedicated to contemporary art and being massively preoccupied with 'relevance' and modernity, the gallery's only permanently exhibited work of art is 2,000 years old. The Berryfield Mosaic was unearthed during construction of the Firstsite gallery. It is a beautiful example of a Roman mosaic, featuring flowers, leaves and elaborate borders.

September 26th

1929: Hollytrees Museum opened its doors to the public on this day. Occupying a 300-year-old building near Colchester Castle, Hollytrees focuses on domestic life and the history of childhood. The house of Hollytrees was built in 1718 and contains timbers from an earlier Tudor house which stood on the site. It passed through various hands over the next couple of centuries, finally being acquired by Colchester Council in 1920. It opened as a museum of 'medieval antiquities and later bygones' nine years later.

Among the exhibits now in the museum are a beautifully constructed doll's house, which is actually a perfect scale model of Hollytrees itself. Other displays show what life would have been like for people of different classes in eighteenth- and nineteenth-century Colchester. Actors often appear dressed in period costume and in character, to bring the past to life for children. In 2000, Hollytrees closed for over a year so that the museum could be completely overhauled. A lift was installed, visitor facilities greatly improved, and the present displays arranged. It is a great museum for families and children.

SEPTEMBER 27TH

1883: On this day, the water tower which became known as Jumbo was completed. It was given this nickname by a disgruntled local vicar whose rectory was overshadowed by the new structure. Coincidentally, the tower, built of 1,200,000 bricks and 800 tons of stone, took twenty months to build; the gestation period of an elephant!

When it was in use, this tower held almost 40,000 cubic feet of water, which was contained in a vast, cast-iron tank. In 1987, a little over a century after it was built, Anglia Water decided that Jumbo was surplus to requirements and sold it. Since then it has changed hands a number of times, although it has never been put to any practical use. On the face of it, Jumbo is an impressive piece of real estate. It is sited in the very heart of Colchester, near the Balkerne Gate. In 2001, planning permission was granted to construct a glass-walled penthouse at the top of the 116ft-high tower. Work never began and the planning permission subsequently lapsed. In 2006, a local developer acquired the property at auction for £330,000. Two years later a charity made plans to restore the tower and open it to the public, although nothing came of these plans.

In September 2011, an application was made for permission to turn Jumbo into flats and a restaurant. This was rejected by Colchester Borough Council and twenty-five years after it stopped being used as a water tower, Jumbo still stands in the heart of Colchester, empty and redundant.

SEPTEMBER 28TH

1962: This is the day that the last section of the Kelvedon and Tollesbury Light Railway closed forever. The line, which became known affectionately as the Crab and Winkle Line, opened in 1904 to provide a link between the main Great Eastern Railway route from London to Colchester and the coast. It ran between the villages of Kelvedon and Tollesbury.

From the beginning, the line was barely used by passengers. The hope when it was built was that a tourist trade might be created, centred around the yachting to be had at Tollesbury. This never happened and the bulk of the traffic on the line was freight; particularly from the jam-making factory at Tiptree. The stops on the line were Kelvedon, Kelvedon Lower Level, Feering Halt, Inworth, Tiptree, Tolleshunt Kinghts, Tolleshun d'Arcy and Tollesbury. Only three of the stops on the line, which was worked by a single engine, had stations – the rest were just low platforms.

The line closed for passengers on May 5th 1951. In October of that year, the entire line closed between Tiptree and Tollesbury, leaving only the short section between Tiptree and Kelvedon open for freight. Eleven years later, this too closed and the Crab and Winkle Line was gone for good.

SEPTEMBER 29TH

2011: There were a good many angry comments on various blogs this day at the news that Tiptree Parish Council had banned the wearing of stiletto heels in the Tiptree Community Centre in Caxton Close.

Letters inviting people to a special event specifically asked them not to wear stiletto heels when attending. The problem was, according to Tiptree councillor Terry Slater, that the centre has a sprung wooden floor and stiletto heels were apt to leave little dimples in it. Ordinary high heels were allowed, said Councillor Webb, but metal-tipped stilettos would cause too much damage.

Some of those commenting on this decision were swift to draw comparisons with the sensitivity lavished upon the cultural needs of minority groups. Nobody actually suggested that it was a religious obligation of Essex girls to wear stilettos, but the general feeling seemed to be that it was all a bit thick. Witham MP Priti Patel and Colchester Mayor Helen Chuah both had no difficulty with the prohibition when they attended the event.

SEPTEMBER 30TH

1349: By this day, 111 wills had been proved in Colchester in the previous twelve months. This compared with an average of two or three a year in the early 1340s. The explanation was a simple one; the Black Death. The Black Death arrived in Colchester in the autumn of 1348 and swept through the town.

The Black Death, which is what bubonic plague was called at that time, reached Europe from Asia in 1347. In 1348, the first cases were reported in this country and it spread rapidly across England in a matter of months. It has been thought that rural Essex was particularly badly affected, with some estimates suggesting that 45 per cent of the population died from the disease. We know that the Abbot and Prior of St John's Abbey in Colchester were dead by August 1349, but to calculate the death toll in the rest of the town we have to fall back on indirect methods. The enormous increase in the number of wills being proved is one way; there are others. The rapid increase in the number of those living and paying Poll Tax in the town in the years following the plague is one clue. Many people flocked to depopulated towns and it is a fact that Colchester's population had increased sharply by the 1360s. Considering how many had been killed by illness just twenty years earlier, this suggests that there were many newcomers, attracted by the opportunities in a thriving town which had been decimated by diseases.

OCTOBER 1ST

2011: On this day, a plaque was unveiled in Colchester's Castle Park, commemorating the ninetieth anniversary of the forming of the Colchester branch of the Royal British Legion. The polished black granite plaque is carved with the badge of the legion and is set in a grey boulder. Colchester Mayor Helen Chuah and branch president Terry Sutton were both present at the unveiling, along with many members of the Royal British Legion. A service of dedication was also held, led by the Legion's Essex chaplain, the Revd Tony Rose.

Colchester is one of the founding members of the Royal British Legion. The British Legion, as it was first known, was founded in 1921 to give a voice to ex-service men and women. It was formed by the merging of four separate organisations; the Comrades of the Great War, the National Association of Discharged Sailors and Soldiers, the National Federation of Discharged and Demobilised Sailors, and Soldiers and the Officers Association. It became the Royal British Legion with the granting of a charter on May 29th 1971, the fiftieth anniversary of the Legion's founding.

OCTOBER 2ND

1931: Sir Thomas Johnson Lipton died on this day. Lipton was the archetypal Victorian rags to riches success story. He had been born to an impoverished Glaswegian family in 1850, signed on as a cabin boy at the age of 14, and then tried his hand at a series of jobs in America before returning to Scotland to start a grocery shop.

Lipton had a great flair for business and Lipton's Tea is famous to this day. As he became a business tycoon, he acquired a taste for yachts, in particular owning them and seeing them entered for competitions. His first yacht was called *Shamrock* and successive yachts were named *Shamrock I*, *Shamrock II* and so on, all the way up to *Shamrock V*. Lipton kept his yachts at Mersea and recruited his crews from either there or Tollesbury. The various incarnations of *Shamrock* were a familiar sight in the Blackwater estuary.

There was generally a strong business end to everything which Thomas Lipton undertook and the yacht racing was no exception. Between 1899 and 1930, his boats tried to win the America's Cup trophy five times. He lost every time, but the attempts on the world title secured him enormous publicity in the USA and stimulated the sales of Lipton's Tea in America.

OCTOBER 3RD

2001: Excavations at St Mary's Hospital in Colchester halted for the season on this day. The digging on the site of the former workhouse revealed a great deal about the Roman suburbs which sprawled beyond the city walls.

It has been known for almost 200 years, since the building of the workhouse outside the Balkerne Gate in fact, that substantial Roman remains lie hidden beneath St Mary's. During the building of the place in the 1830s, it was recorded that the foundations of at least three masonry buildings were uncovered and, even more excitingly, a peculiar square within a square building – almost without doubt a Romano-Celtic temple.

The 2001 dig unearthed a number of burials from the Roman period. These were not packed closely together, but rather scattered over a large area. Most were straightforward burials, although one or two were the remains of cremations. Three buildings were excavated, including one of great interest, with a cellar which had been filled with the debris from the demolition of a house which once stood here. The original structure had been of mud bricks which had been covered with painted plaster – it was a stark reminder that not all Romans lived in grand, marble palaces.

OCTOBER 4TH

1939: Construction of an anti-tank ditch at Shrub End in Colchester began on this day. From 1938 onwards, efforts were made to fortify the east coast of Britain, especially Essex, against invasion from Germany. Part of this work consisted in the building of concrete pill boxes, many of which are still to be found in the county's fields. They were essentially machine gun nests, which would have slowed down the invading force. These might have proved effective against light infantry, but they would have been wholly useless against tanks.

Working on the assumption that German armour would be used in an invasion to secure the major towns of Essex, just as in the blitzkrieg attacks on Poland and France, attempts were made to prevent the German *panzers* from getting too close to Colchester. These precautions mirror eerily the ditches and dykes which the ancient Britons dug around Camulodunum in order to prevent enemy chariots from getting too close for comfort. Blocks of concrete, so called tank-traps, and deep ditches across strategic parts of the open country were scattered across the landscape. It is open to question just how effective these defence would have proved.

OCTOBER 5TH

2011: The SAVE Trust, whose interest is the preservation of old buildings, visited Colchester on this day to discuss the implications of their report, 'Colchester: Back to the Future' (2010).

SAVE's report expressed itself forcefully about the need for Colchester to take care of the old buildings in the town, rather than allowing them to be swept aside in the rush to create new ones. As they put it:

> The town must capitalise on its history and heritage, rather than bend to the concrete will of those who mistakenly believe that economic development and physical development are one and the same. Only through conserving and, where possible, carefully adding to the town, can Colchester strengthen and retain its real identity.

The Colchester and North East Essex Building Preservation Trust, who hosted the visit, were keen to endorse SAVE's report by targeting a number of threatened local buildings and recommending them for preservation. Among these were the Jumbo water tower and Tymperley's, an ancient building in the town which formely housed a museum.

OCTOBER 6TH

1700: Philip Morant was born in Jersey on this day. He studied at both Oxford and Cambridge, before being ordained into the Church of England in 1722. He held various posts, including that of chaplain in the Dutch city of Amsterdam, before moving to Essex in 1737. He was appointed Rector of both St Mary-at-the-Walls church in Colchester and also of the village of Aldham.

Morant is best known today for his work on the history of Essex; he has been described as the first historian of the county. In 1748, he published *The History and Antiquities of Colchester*; the first comprehensive study of the town's history. Between 1763 and 1768 he published *The History and Antiquities of Essex* in two volumes. His investigations into the history of Essex were not limited to research and writing. He was the first to excavate and examine systematically some of the Roman sites in and near to Colchester. As a result of these activities, he was elected to the Fellowship of the Society of Antiquaries in London in 1755.

Morant's books are still a valuable source of information about the county of Essex. Ironically, his historical research is less valuable than the light which he sheds on the state of the county in his own time.

OCTOBER 7TH

1962: The distinctive logo of the Colchester Lathe Company was registered as a trademark on this day. It shows the motto 'The World Turns on Colchester Lathes' encircling a globe. The Colchester Lathe Company was founded by John Ephrain Cohen in 1887, although the name of the company was not actually registered until 1907.

The First World War gave the company a great boost, with the demand for cheap and effective machinery in armaments factories. It was not for another thirty years or so that it became a limited company in 1949. It was in the 1960s that the Colchester Lathe Company became an international concern, following the building of a new factory in Elmstead Road. It was soon winning the Queen's Award to Industry regularly for various aspects of its work – primarily those concerned with overseas trade.

The Colchester Lathe Company was a big local employer throughout the 1970s and '80s and it was something of a shock when, in 1992, the company announced that it was moving lock, stock and barrel to the West Yorkshire town of Heckmonwike.

OCTOBER 8TH

1949: Sigourney Weaver, the American film star, was born on this day. Her mother, the actress Elizabeth Inglis, was born in Colchester. Elizabeth Inglis was born Desiree Mary Lucy Hawkins in 1913. Her mother's maiden name was Inglis, which explains her later stage name.

Elizabeth Inglis was drawn to Hollywood, like so many other hopeful young actresses in the 1920s and '30s. Unlike many, she was successful in breaking into the movies, her first film being *Borrowed Clothes*, made in 1934. The following year she had a part in Alfred Hithcock's classic version of John Buchan's story *The 39 Steps*.

In 1942, Elizabeth Inglis married Sylvester Weaver, a radio executive who later became president of NBC. Sigourney was one of the two children from this marriage. After marrying Weaver, Elizabeth retired completely from acting and devoted herself to her family. She was still living in California when she died in 2007 at the age of 95. She had been the last surviving member of the cast of *The 39 Steps*.

OCTOBER 9TH

1318: This was the first mention of the annual St Denis' Fair, which was held in Colchester. Across Europe there was a custom of holding fairs at about this time of year, it was probably because this time of year marked the end of the harvest and was a time when agricultural workers had a little money in their pockets and a certain amount of free time once the harvest was safely gathered in.

Colchester's St Denis' Fair was held on the site of Colchester's present-day bus station. The first written mention of this fair is from 1318. Craftsmen came from all over the county to sell their wares at the market, which lasted for a week. During that time, stalls were set up and these doubled as makeshift shelters under which men slept at night. It was a time when the normal rules were relaxed a little and drunkenness and good humour reigned. By the end of the harvest, many tools such as knives and spades, buckets and leather belts were all getting a little worn out. Since men had a little spare money, it was the time to combine business with pleasure and to kit oneself out for the winter months ahead.

OCTOBER 10TH

1654: The hereditary title of Viscount of Colchester passed on this date to John Savage. Colchester has had two noble titles associated with it; there have been both a Viscount and Baron Colchester, although neither title are now in existence.

The first Viscount of Colchester was Thomas Savage, at one time Baron Darcy of Chiche and later Earl Rivers. If all these titles sound confusing, this is not to be wondered at – even professional genealogists have trouble keeping track of the various successions involved in the British aristocracy. The Viscountcy of Colchester was created for the then Baron Darcy of Chiche and conferred upon him on July 5th 1621. On his death in February 1639, the Barony of Darcy of Chiche became extinct, but the Viscountcy of Colchester passed to his grandson, along with the title of Earl Rivers.

John Savage, the 5th Earl Rivers, subsequently inherited the title of Viscount of Colchester, but the succession hit a full stop when he was ordained as a Catholic priest in 1712. Since Catholic priests are celibate, this meant that both the Earldom and Viscountcy died with him on May 9th 1736.

OCTOBER 11TH

1899: The Boers declared war against Britain on this day.

The Boers, descendants of Dutch settlers in Africa, were contesting the British for control of the area which became known as South Africa. At the declaration of war, the 2nd Battalion Royal Irish Fusiliers were based in Colchester. The expectation was that the war would be over so soon that they would not even have time to reach Africa. In the event, the fighting dragged on for an incredible three years, before the British were able to capture the whole of South Africa.

A crucial action of the war concerned the siege of Ladysmith – a town which contained a vital rail junction. Members of the 1st Battalion Irish Fusiliers were taken prisoner and detained at Ladysmith, while the 3rd Battalion besieged the town and tried in vain to free their comrades. The siege of Ladysmith became front page news in England and a reminder that the British did not always have everything all their own way, even at the height of Empire.

The 2nd Battalion Irish Fusiliers were despatched from Colchester and it was they who finally broke the siege and entered Ladysmith in 1900.

OCTOBER 12TH

1841: A report was made to the House of Commons on this day about the conditions in English prisons. Colchester Castle had not been used as a prison for a few years and a new House of Correction had been built in Colchester. It stood on the Ipswich Road.

Only twenty-five or thirty prisoners were held in the Colchester House of Correction at any one time. Unusually, it was a mixed prison; there always seemed to have been a few women as well as men being held there. The commonest offence for which people were committed to the place was vagrancy; this one crime accounted for over half the people who were confined there in 1840 and 1841.

The Punishment Book records various breaches of discipline and the resulting penalties. For such trifling violations as talking during exercise, a prisoner could be deprived of his next meal or locked in his cell for twenty-four hours.

The great majority of those held at Colchester were young men under 30 and at least two thirds of them were unable to read and write. Those under 21, however, received an hours' tuition a day in this. Surprisingly, whipping was still in use; two young men having received this punishment over the course of the year.

OCTOBER 13TH

54: On this day the Roman emperor Claudius died. In AD 43 the Romans arrived in Britain, intending to turn this island into a colony of Rome. At that time, London was no more than a malarial swamp and so the Roman army advanced on the biggest settlement in the south of the country, which happened to be Colchester.

Where present-day Colchester stands was a Celtic town called Camulodunum. It was in effect the capital of southern Britain. An army of 40,000 Romans arrived at Camulodunum and then halted to await their emperor before entering the town. When Claudius landed from France, he brought with him some war elephants and these accompanied him to Camulodunum. They must have been an awe-inspiring sight to the Britons.

Claudius stayed only sixteen days in Britain; just long enough to accept the surrender of ten kings and one queen. The Roman's built their first city at Camulodunum and for the first fifteen years of their occupation, this served as the provincial capital.

OCTOBER 14TH

1948: *Flight* magazine carried an article this day about seaplanes. For those unfamiliar with the subject, these are aeroplanes designed to take off and land on water. The piece in *Flight* is intriguing because it claims that the first British seaplane operated at Wivenhoe before the First World War. It is a brief mention and reads in full:

> Indeed, although British aquatic aviation goes back to 1909 when the first crude seaplane appeared at Wivenhoe, it was not until the 1938 *Ark Royal* that a warship appeared basically designed as an aircraft carrier.

In December 1955, *Flight* clarified this bald and surprising statement. It turned out that while a seaplane had been moored off Wivenhoe in 1909, it had never actually flown and was almost certainly incapable of flight!

Instead of wheels, seaplanes have floats which enable them to behave like boats on the water. *Flight* magazine said of the mysterious Wivenhoe seaplane in 1955:

> The earliest recorded British attempt to produce an aeroplane capable of rising from the water was the Rawson-Barton Hydra-aeroplane of 1905. It did not fly, nor did the improbable structure designed by Mr Jack Humphreysand built at Wivenhoe in 1909.

The question of whether or not Wivenhoe can justifiably be called the birthplace of the seaplane remains an open one.

OCTOBER 15TH

1733: John Kay started a partnership in Colchester on this day to promote the use of a new type of shuttle for weaving which he had invented. He could not have known it at the time, but this partnership could be called the start of Britain's Industrial Revolution.

Colchester had been a centre for weaving since at least the fourteenth century. Until the eighteenth century, weaving was essentially a cottage industry, with the manufacture taking place in the homes of weavers. John Kay's new shuttle, which became known as the flying shuttle, threatened to change all that. To begin with, it increased productivity enormously, but it also meant that fewer workers were needed. With the old hand shuttles, one person pushed the shuttle across the loom and another caught it on the other side. Kay's flying shuttle was faster and needed only one person to operate it. It didn't take long for the idea of rows of looms operated together in a special building to emerge; the first factories in other words.

Colchester's weavers were not pleased to find somebody trying to disrupt the traditional way of life which they had been enjoying for centuries and by September they were petitioning the King to suppress Kay's invention. He later moved to Leeds, thus precipitating its grown as a manufacturing centre.

OCTOBER 16TH

2010: On this day, the Colchester Natural History Society held its annual 'Fungus Foray'. Rather disloyally, they chose to take the participants not only out of the borough of Colchester, but out of the county entirely to Rendlesham Forest in Suffolk. The expedition to Suffolk was by coach and open to anybody; not just members of the Colchester Natural History Society. Later that year, on October 31st, another such trip took place – this time to Wivenhoe Woods.

It is doubtful whether anybody but the dedicated natural history enthusiast can fully understand the attraction of traipsing around woods in the autumn looking for toadstools and mushrooms. These days, one is not allowed even to pick the fungi and so ventures of this sort are usually restricted to examining fungus *in situ* and perhaps taking the odd photograph. Still, judging by the fact that this is an annual event in the calendar of those in Colchester devoted to natural history, we must assume that the enterprise has its compensations.

OCTOBER 17TH

1998: Joan Hickson, the actress famous for her portrayal of Agatha Christie's Miss Marple, died on this day. She had lived in Rose Lane, Wivenhoe for forty years.

Born in 1906, Joan was a talented and versatile actress, starring in many films and plays. In the 1940s she acted in *Appointment with Death*, a play by Agatha Christie. After watching the play, the author sent her a note saying, 'I hope one day you will play my dear Miss Marple'. It was to be forty years before the opportunity came Joan's way.

In the early 1980s, the BBC decided to produce new versions of Agatha Christie's novels for the television. At that time Joan was almost 80, but she was keen to accept the challenge of the role when it was offered to her. She played Miss Marple in twelve television adaptations of Agatha Christie novels between 1984 and 1992. She was an astonishing 86 by the time the series had finished. A plaque has recently been placed on the house in Wivenhoe where she lived from 1958 until her death in 1998.

OCTOBER 18TH

1926: On this day, Klaus Gunter Karl Nakszynski was born in the city of Danzig. He became better known as Klaus Kinski, the film actor who appeared in a number of films by the director Werner Herzog.

Of part German and part Polish ancestry, in 1943 Kinski was conscripted into the German army. He was captured by the British in 1944 and shipped back to England as a prisoner of war. He was interned at Camp 186 at Berechurch Hall in Colchester.

It was while being held prisoner by the British that Kinski discovered that he had a talent for acting. He took part in theatrical performances intended to raise the morale of the prisoners. When the war in Europe ended, Kinski was desperate to be repatriated to his own country. The policy at that time was that sick prisoners would be sent back to Germany first, so, in order to make himself ill, Kinski took to standing outside the barracks all night without any clothes on, as well as drinking his own urine and eating tobacco. Unfortunately for him, he remained in good health and was not allowed home until 1946.

Acting seemingly ran in Kinski's blood, because his daughter Nastassja also became an actress, starring in such films as Roman Polanski's *Tess*.

OCTOBER 19TH

1836: This is the day that the Colchester Poor Law Union came into being. This resulted in the setting up of the Union Workhouses so hated by the poor and mercilessly caricatured and lampooned by Charles Dickens in books such as *Oliver Twist*.

The new Poor Law was created following the perception by some in the early nineteenth century that the existing workhouses were places of idleness and entertainment. As Dickens put it, 'It was a regular place of public entertainment for the poorer classes; a tavern where there was nothing to pay; a public breakfast, dinner and tea with nothing to pay; a brick and mortar Elysium, where it was all play and no work'. The aim of the new workhouses was that nobody should be able to have more to eat than the poorest person who actually was working. Since many working people constantly lived on the edge of starvation, conditions in workhouses were grim indeed.

Many workhouses were later converted to hospitals. A few buildings of the old Colchester Workhouse still remain.

OCTOBER 20TH

1941: This is the day that the army's No. 2 Motor Boat Company moved to Mersea Island. After the fall of France in 1940 and the evacuation of the British army from Dunkirk, there was a very real fear of a German invasion across the English Channel. Even when this danger had passed, there was an anxiety that the Germans might try to land agents to carry out acts of sabotage.

No. 2 Motor Boat Company was formed in Gloucestershire in 1940 and then moved to Mersea the following year. Most of their work consisted of patrolling the estuaries of the rivers Colne and Blackwater. These would have been ideal places for spies and saboteurs to land and it was a prudent precaution to keep a watch on this part of the coast facing France. The fact that Mersea was a yachting and boating centre helped the work of this unit – which was part of the Army Service Corps – immeasurably. There were already harbours and berths for any number of small boats on the island.

The units saw no real action while based at Mersea and the most exciting mission they ever undertook was to search for the survivors of a British plane which crashed nearby in 1943.

OCTOBER 21ST

1905: The Britannia Engineering Company in Colchester published on this day their catalogue of cars which they were manufacturing. This was in the days before a few large companies dominated the field and there were a number of small British firms trying to break into the motor car industry.

Behind Colchester Town railway station is a car park and it was here that the Britannia Works once stood. Its association with metal-working stretched back to 1811, when an Irishman called William Dearn was making nails here. His son expanded the business into an iron foundry and then into the production of sewing machines. At this time, the firm was called the Britannia Sewing Machine Company. By the 1870s, they had stopped making sewing machines and had branched out into drills and bicycles.

In 1893, the company, still operating on the original site, began making oil engines. These were not a success and, after limping along for another decade, the business was sold to Victor, Hugh and Percy Nicholson. They decided that the future lay in cars and began producing the Britannia range of four cylinder cars. These were offered with a six-month guarantee on all the materials used. Although the cars themselves were sound enough, there was not a great enough market and the Britannia cars were no longer manufactured after 1908.

OCTOBER 22ND

1536: William More was consecrated as the first Bishop of Colchester on this day. He owed his elevation to this newly created position more to Henry VIII's marital difficulties than any qualities he himself possessed.

Henry had determined to get rid of his first wife, Catherine of Aragon, and replace her with his mistress, Anne Boleyn. Unfortunately, the Catholic Church was opposed to divorce and refused to annul his marriage. His solution was dramatic; he abandoned the Catholic Church and started his own church – the Church of England. This meant a hasty reorganisation of the existing bishops and priests. Those who were too firmly wedded to Rome's line were removed and replaced with others who were more amenable to the King's wishes.

Before being appointed bishop, William More had held a few minor posts in Essex, being for a time Rector of Bradwell. He must have proved satisfactory to the powers that be, because he remained Bishop of Colchester until his death in 1541. It must be supposed that he possessed the happy knack of going along with whatever Henry VIII decided in the religious line. Several abbots in the Colchester did not have this ability and ended up being executed for treason.

OCTOBER 23RD

2010: This was Apple Day throughout the entire country and it was marked by a number of local events in the Colchester area.

The festival of Apple Day was apparently launched in Covent garden in 1990 and the aim is to have a day in the calendar when we celebrate that most popular and quintessentially English of fruits. Some of the activities organised, however, sound a little odd. Afghanaid, for example, asked people to organise 'Apples for Afghanistan' parties to raise money for refugees in that country. The connection between Afghanistan and apples seemed at best tenuous; it being claimed that the fruit originated in the Tien Shan Mountains, 500 miles north of Afghanistan.

In Colchester, a celebration of the apple began at Crapes Fruit Farm, on Rectory Road, Aldham, with a display of hundreds of different varieties of apples. Visitors were encouraged to bring their own apples to be identified by the experts at Crapes Fruit Farm and were offered the chance to taste some types of apple with which they might not have been familiar. It was also possible to order packs of various types as Christmas and birthday presents.

OCTOBER 24TH

2011: A Colchester paratrooper from 16 Air Assault Brigade appeared at Manchester Crown Court on this day charged in connection with looting during the riots which swept the country in August 2011. Twenty-year-old Gunner Liam Bretherton was on leave when the riots struck his home town of Manchester. On August 9th, which also happened to be his birthday, he headed into the centre of town to see what was happening. He ended up at a music shop, which had been plundered by a mob. Bretherton then paid a stranger £20 for a guitar which the man had just stolen from the shop.

What Bretherton could not possibly have known, not being a guitar aficionado, was that this was no ordinary guitar. To begin with it was a very good make; a Gibson Les Paul. Not only that, but it was extremely noticeable, due to the fact that it was actually a left-handed guitar. When he tried to dispose of it at a music shop a couple of days later, the shopkeeper was immediately suspicious as to what this young man was doing with a guitar worth thousands of pounds. Bretherton was sent to a Young Offenders Institution for eight months.

OCTOBER 25TH

1894: Colchester's first public lending library opened in West Stockwell Street on this day. Although built in the Victorian era, the building itself was designed to look Jacobean. It has the appearance of a baronial hall, with a ceiling covered in wooden beams.

The concept of a 'lending' library dates from the nineteenth century. Before then, libraries were scholarly places, where people went to consult books which were too rare or expensive for them to have any hope of acquiring for themselves. The lending library was a different thing entirely. When the library in West Stockwell Street first opened it had, in addition to 1,310 reference books which remained on the premises at all times, a stock of 3,324 books – including popular novels – which members of the library could take home with them.

In an age when there were no such things as cheap paperbacks, most working people could not afford to buy books for their own use. The public lending libraries thus opened up the world of literature to the ordinary man in the street.

OCTOBER 26TH

1803: On this day, King George III reviewed volunteers in London, a number of whom were from Essex regiments. This was at the height of the Napoleonic Wars and Colchester's position as a garrison town really dates from then. 1803 was a crucial year in the protracted wars in which England was entangled, and fear of invasion from the continent was very real. Colchester was particularly badly hit by the invasion panic. According to contemporary accounts, soldiers were 'pouring in daily' to the town.

Any invasion of England would of course have involved troops landing on the East coast and this made East Essex, in a sense, the front line. Those who could afford to do so left the town and headed west to Bath and other safer and perhaps more fashionable locations. Colchester was an armed camp and it was pretty clear that if the French did land, then there would be fierce fighting on the beaches around Mersea and Wivenhoe. The air of crisis could not have been helped when the Prince of Orange, whose own country of Holland was occupied by the French, arrived in Colchester with a hundred of his soldiers. The sight of foreign troops in their town would hardly have been a comforting one for the citizens of Colchester.

OCTOBER 27TH

1967: The Nottage Maritime Institute was registered as a charity on this day. It had actually been around since 1896, being founded that year by Captain Charles Nottage as a place where those living by the River Colne could, 'improve themselves in navigation primarily, or make up their skills generally'. Essentially, it was to be a shore-based school for sailors, teaching all the skills that sailors, fishermen, yachtsmen and anybody else putting out to sea would find useful.

To begin with, the Nottage Institute operated from a three-storey building next to the Black Buoy pub. It moved in 1947 to its present location on Wivenhoe Quay. The Nottage serves these days as a maritime library and heritage museum, but the practical skills of seamanship have not been neglected. Evening classes are still held here in navigation and other skills. Most of the students these days tend to be weekend sailors rather than those who make their living from the sea. The ground floor of the institute is devoted entirely to teaching the construction of traditional, clinker-built dinghies. Captain Nottage's legacy still thrives in Wivenhoe and shows no sign of fading away any time soon.

OCTOBER 28TH

1909: Francis Bacon was born in Dublin on this day. Recognised as one of the greatest British artists of his generation, he lived mainly in England from his teenage years onwards. In the early 1950s, Bacon acquired a cottage in Wivenhoe, a few miles south-east of Colchester. He lived and worked in the village for much of the next twenty years or so.

Many people are aware that St Ives in Cornwall is a popular artists' colony; few know that Wivenhoe also has a thriving artistic scene. A number of professional artists have made their home in the town and painting is a popular local hobby. Francis Bacon did not altogether fit into the Wivenhoe community of artists. Possibly his heavy drinking and openly homosexual lifestyle were to blame, but the fact is that he was banned from the local art club; an extraordinary thing to happen to a man whom many regard as the finest painter in this country since Constable!

The cottage which Bacon owned in Wivenhoe has remained precisely as it was upon his death in 1992.

OCTOBER 29TH

1835: On this day, the last prisoner left Colchester Castle and it was never again used as a prison. The earliest record of the castle being used as a prison was in 1226 and it was, until 1667, the county prison.

Some of the early prisoners in the castle are, to say the least, a little surprising. In 1296, for instance, the vicar of Coggeshall was locked up for fishing in Coggeshall Abbey fishponds! Through the sixteenth and seventeenth centuries, the prison contained what we would today regard as political prisoners; men and women whose only offence was adherence to the 'wrong' religion or membership of the 'wrong' faction in one of the civil wars or rebellions which racked the country. Conditions in the cells were pretty dreadful. The castle was dilapidated and the roof leaked badly. During one fierce storm in 1646, the prisoners were forced to stand all night in water which came up to their knees.

By the late eighteenth century, conditions had improved somewhat and the prison was less crowded than it had once been. In 1788, building work was carried out which meant that there were cells for just two women and three men. Strict new rules were introduced on prison accommodation in 1824, and this more or less spelled the end of the castle as a prison.

OCTOBER 30TH

1892: Castle Park in Colchester opened on this day. It is listed as Grade II on the Register of Historic Parks and Gardens of Special Historic Interest in England. Covering twenty-four acres in the centre of Colchester, with the castle at its heart, Castle Park is one of the most popular places in the town to relax.

The park was originally much smaller than it is today. The year after it was opened, more land was added and still more in 1896. In 1920, the grounds of Hollytrees mansion, now a museum, were acquired, bringing the park to its present size. Proposals for a park in this area were first put forward in 1870, but the council first had to negotiate the purchase of the land. Today, the park contains just about everything which one would hope to find in a municipal park: flowerbeds, lawns, swings, a cricket ground and boating lake. Castle Park regularly wins awards and in 2009, for instance, it was officially named as being 'Britain's Best Park'. Castle Park fought of stiff competition from across the nation to win the title, awarded by lawnmower manufacturer Briggs & Stratton.

OCTOBER 31ST

2010: Peter Hoskin, writing in the blog of the magazine *The Spectator*, related a curious incident on this day about Colchester's MP. Apparently, Bob Russell was so angry about the Coalition Government's planned cuts in Housing Benefit that he was granted a private meeting with Nick Clegg; the Deputy Prime Minister. After receiving no assurances from Clegg that he would reconsider the Liberal position and oppose the proposed cuts, Bob Russell stormed out of the Commons committee room, slamming the door behind him so hard that it came off its hinges.

A friend of Mr Russell's and fellow MP, Mike Hancock, supposedly turned up at the committee room very early the following morning and mended the door before House of Commons staff had a chance to spot the damage. It is only fair to say that Bob Russell denied that anything of the sort happened. He claimed that the whole thing was just a Westminster joke which was going the rounds.

NOVEMBER 1ST

2000: This is the day that St Helen's chapel in Colchester became an Orthodox place of worship. The chapel, in Maidenburgh Street, just off the High Street, is probably the oldest place of worship in Colchester. Its foundations are built into the remains of the Roman theatre, which argues that it predates the Saxon period.

When the Normans began building their castle in Colchester in 1076, they undertook the restoration of St Helen's, suggesting that it was already at that time very old and in need of repair. In the fifteenth century a chantry was attached to the chapel, and it was this which caused the place to fall into disuse in the centuries following Henry VIII's dissolution of the monasteries. The presence of a chantry suggested to those in power during the Reformation that here was a symbol of Roman Catholicism and that, as such, it was better done away with. Over the succeeding centuries it was used as a school, workshop, library and house. It was not until the 1880s that it was restored as a church.

For a while, St Helen's functioned as a parish hall and then became used as a storeroom. In 1999, the Orthodox Church came to an agreement with the Church of England and St Helen's was once again used for worship.

NOVEMBER 2ND

1914: On this day, Camille Coquette, a Belgian soldier, died. His grave is to be found in Colchester Cemetery. The cemetery contains a special section for war graves, which include those of soldiers of many nationalities who fought alongside the British army. Coquette died in the opening moths of the First World War, following the German invasion of his country in August 1914. It is assumed that he was wounded and then brought back to England, where he died. His is one of a row of four neat headstones, all identical and marked with the colours of the Belgian flag. Because he was a Catholic and buried in an Anglican cemetery, Camille Coquette was, in effect, interred in unconsecrated ground.

There is a very sad story associated with Coquette's death. Although the English made every effort to provide a fitting funeral for the four Belgian soldiers, due to an administrative oversight, Coquette was listed in the cemetery records as 'an unknown Belgian soldier'. After the end of the First World War, in 1918, his mother scoured Belgium, trying to find out what had happened to her son. Although his name is engraved upon the headstone, there is no other record of this soldier in this country and so all enquiries from Belgium were returned with the information that nothing was known about the man.

NOVEMBER 3RD

1870: In the by-election held on this day, Alexander Learmonth became the new MP for Colchester. The run-up to the election was marked by a campaign against the notorious Contagious Diseases Acts, and Josephine Butler, a well known and vociferous campaigner against the Acts, visited Colchester during the election.

Because most men in the army were unmarried, much use was made of prostitutes, particularly in garrison towns like Colchester. As a result of this, many soldiers contracted diseases such as syphilis. The government's answer was to pass a law in 1864 allowing for the compulsory testing of prostitutes for venereal diseases and also for their detention in hospitals to prevent them from spreading disease among soldiers. It was monstrously unfair to focus in this way upon the prostitutes rather than their clients and in some towns, women who were not prostitutes found themselves being taken off to police stations and forced to undergo intimate examinations.

What made the Colchester election so important was that an attempt was being made to extend the scope of the Contagious Diseases Acts from just garrison towns and ports to the entire country. The Acts were finally repealed in 1885.

NOVEMBER 4TH

1867: Henry Charles Fehr was born on this day. He was a well-known sculptor in his day and specialised in monumental, allegorical figures in bronze. Perhaps his most famous work was the war memorial in Colchester, which was unveiled in 1923.

A case can be made for the Colchester war memorial being the most beautiful in the whole country. The main figure, a dramatic, 11-foot high statue of Victory, stands on a 17-foot high pedestal of Portland Stone. Two smaller figures, also cast in bronze and both 7 feet high, flank the pedestal on either side. One is of St George in full armour, the other represents peace in the form of a woman holding a dove. The memorial stands near Colchester Castle and a number of old buildings were demolished to make room for it. The intention was that this awe-inspiring piece of work should be clearly visible from the High Street.

The man responsible for creating the war memorial evidently agreed with the choice of location. Addressing a group of local councillors, Henry Fehr said, 'I believe if you were to search all England you would not find a more suitable or more beautiful site for a War Memorial Monument than the one you have got. It is an ideal site.'

NOVEMBER 5TH

2010: The *Ipswich Star* reported on this day that Colchester Borough Council had voted in favour of setting up a site for a Gypsy camp in Colchester. The site, which would have pitches for twelve caravans, was to be on Severalls Lane in North Colchester.

There was strong local opposition to the establishment of the site from those living nearby. The point was made that there were no available school places in the area and that Severalls Lane was already very busy and that any extra traffic was undesirable. The owner of a nearby factory claimed that there had already been break-ins on his premises, with the intruders seemingly searching for scrap metal. He suggested that this sort of offence would become more prevalent if a permanent site for Travellers was set up in the area.

Speaking in favour of the site at the meeting, Jan Plummer from Tendring and Colchester Ethnic Minority Partnership denied that there was any evidence that there was a higher level of crime in the vicinity of Gypsy camps. The Planning Committee voted eleven to one in favour of the proposal.

NOVEMBER 6TH

1922: On this day, one of the most important archaeological treasures of Colchester was uncovered by accident. Mr A.W. Frost lived on North Hill and he was digging in his kitchen garden, when his spade struck what he took to be a stony patch. When he started to clear what he at first took to be small pebbles from the rich earth, he found that they were actually little cubes of stone; cubes that had clearly been deliberately shaped. He stopped digging and began to sweep the soil from the area with his hands. It did not take him long to realise that he had struck not a random pile of little tesserae, the tiles used by the Romans to construct their mosaic, but an intact example, laying only a foot or two beneath his garden.

Today, the North Hill mosaic may be seen just inside the entrance to the Colchester Museum in the castle. It is a complex geometric pattern of red, white and black cubes, which dates from about AD 150. It was probably laid in the reception room of a luxurious townhouse, when Roman Colchester was at its height. Had Mr Frost not been such an enthusiastic gardener, it might never have been discovered.

NOVEMBER 7TH

1885: The lndlord of the Barley Mow public house on Hythe Hill, near Colchester, fired a revolver at the barmaid who lived on the premises on this day. Robert Hay was 60 and he had engaged 23-year-old Alice Ashenton to work at the pub. It is an age-old story. At first the landlord seemingly wished to treat the young woman as a daughter, but within a short time he had proposed to her. She declined his offer and he grew angry and bitterly jealous of a younger man, whom his barmaid evidently favoured over and above himself.

In the early hours of November 7th, Hay staggered into Alice's room, clearly the worse for drink. He was brandishing a pistol, which went off, wounding the young woman in the head. By some miracle, she was not killed, but Hay was arrested and charged with attempted murder. When locked in a cell at the police station, he tried to hang himself with torn up sheets from the bed.

At the trial, Alice spoke on Hay's behalf. She repeatedly told the court that, 'although he shot me, he had no intention to harm me'. The jury chose to consider the affair an unfortunate accident. There is no record of what became of the principle figures in the case. The Barley Mow was demolished in 1972.

NOVEMBER 8TH

2010: This day was the premiere of a play by local writer Paul T. Davies, performed at Colchester's Headgate Theatre. *The Green Room* is the story, delivered through three monologues, of an aging theatrical agent who falls in love with a boy whose career he is promoting.

The Headgate Theatre, opened in 2002, is Colchester's lesser known place to see contemporary plays. Everybody knows about the Mercury, near the Balkerne Gate, but not everyone has heard of the Headgate. It is in a converted Baptist chapel, which was built in Chapel Street in 1844. In the 1980s, a group of local people set up Theatre Arts Action, with the hope of establishing a theatre which could put on amateur productions. After a long search, Colchester Council agreed to buy the then derelict chapel for them and give them a twenty-five year lease on the place. They would have to raise almost a quarter of a million pounds themselves though, in order to do it up. By getting a grant from the National Lottery and some very active fundraising elsewhere, the money was raised and in 2002 the Headgate Theatre put on its first play.

NOVEMBER 9TH

1888: A crane was shot at Elmstead, a village near Colchester, on this day. Apparently, on November 9th, some large birds were observed in a field near Elmstead Hall Farm. Inevitably, somebody started shooting at them and the result was that a large but immature specimen was bagged. This was taken to a Mr Pettitt, a taxidermist in Colchester, to be stuffed. *The Essex Naturalist* – the journal of the Essex Field Club – gives a detailed description of the birds, noting that it was a common crane, but with immature plumage – the characteristic red mark on the head was missing. After the animal had been stuffed, it was presented to the Saffron Walden Museum. It was apparently the first crane ever killed in the county.

The crane is a rare migrant to this country today, but there is reason to believe that it once lived and bred here in fairly large numbers. An Act of Parliament in 1533 made it an offence to take cranes' eggs, which suggests that they were present in England at that time. There is a slight difficulty in being sure about this though, because the grey heron was often called a crane in country districts.

NOVEMBER 10TH

1801: John Moore died on this day and left a legacy for poor people living near St Peter's Church at the top of North Hill in Colchester. By today's standards, the sum was modest enough; just £200. The stated intention in Moore's will was that the money should be invested and the interest used annually to buy bread, coals and other necessities of life for poor people. Moore's legacy is inscribed upon a marble tablet, which includes details of other benefactors to the poor who had been associated with St Peter's. Jeremiah Daniel, for example, left money to pay for some coats for the poor.

There is a curious postscript to John Moore's benevolent action. Beneath the account of his legacy has been added, at a later date, the curt information that 'This legacy produced only £82.15s.2d'. There is no explanation for this and nothing of the sort is said about the end results of the other money which was similarly left. £200 would have been a pretty considerable amount of money 200 years ago and it should have continued to earn a reasonable rate of interest for many years. We shall probably never know.

NOVEMBER 11TH

2010: Three students from the University of Essex were arrested in London on this day during national protests about the raising of university tuition fees.

The protest march had been well organised and the route agreed beforehand by the Metropolitan Police. Unfortunately, the police seriously underestimated the number of students who would be turning up for the demonstration. They thought that only 20,000 or so would turn up; in fact over 50,000 arrived from all over the country and as far away as Wales. A convoy of six coaches arrived from the Wivenhoe campus of the University of Essex, containing 300 students and lecturers.

The march was scheduled to pass the Houses of Parliament and culminate in a rally at the Tate Gallery on Millbank. It did not seem to have occurred to anybody that the headquarters of the Conservative Party were also on Millbank. The building was stormed and a lot of vandalism carried out. Protestors gathered on the roof to chant slogans. The police tactic was to evacuate staff and then cordon off the building. They then began letting the students out one at a time and arresting those whom they supposed to have been engaged in acts of vandalism. It was at this point that the three students from Essex were detained.

NOVEMBER 12TH

1861: On this day, Charles Dickens gave readings from some of his books in Colchester. It was not the first time that he had visited the town. In 1835, as a young reporter, he had covered elections in East Anglia and had formed no good opinion of the area. While staying in Chelmsford, for instance, he found that all the shops closed on Sunday and so he was unable to buy a newspaper. He described it as, 'the dullest and most stupid place on Earth'. he didn't think much of Colchester and other towns when he visited them in the same year, writing that he 'came away with no better opinion of any of them'. Harsh words indeed!

In 1861, when he was one of the most famous men in England, Dickens travelled around Britain giving readings from his books. His workload at this time would have been enough to exhaust a much younger man and it is thought that these public readings helped to wreck his health and contribute to his death. In the days before reaching Colchester, he had performed at Bury St Edmunds, Ipswich and Norwich; at which places he read selections primarily from *David Copperfield*.

NOVEMBER 13TH

2011: An unusual screening of the film *Arthur Christmas* took place in the Colchester Odeon and fifty other cinemas across the country on this day. The film was shown in an 'autism friendly' environment. Some people with autism find that their senses are far more acute than other people. This can mean that loud noises are unbearable and some visual stimulation can cause distress. In an ordinary cinema production of course, these are precisely the features which most people seek. They sit in a darkened auditorium and are dazzled by brilliant colours. The sound is overpowering and the film itself is preceded by exciting and eye-catching advertisements and trailers for new films.

The autism friendly screenings take place with the lights turned up and the sound down. Those watching can move about the place if it makes them feel more comfortable and there are no confusing and distracting trailers of advertisements. There is also no objection to patrons making noises if it helps them to appreciate the film. The screening at the Colchester Odeon was a great success and there are plans to repeat the event.

NOVEMBER 14TH

1916: General Horace William Montagu died at Colchester on this day. He must surely rank as the archetypal career soldier.

Montagu was born in 1823, the son of the Reverend George Montagu and Emily Yonge. He joined the army as an officer at a very young age and fought in the Crimean War. He was awarded the Order of Merit of Sardinia for his actions there and was also invested as a Knight, Legion of Honour. After the end of the Crimean War, he married Catherine Frances England on August 4th 1859. She was the only daughter of General Poole England.

Montagu rose steadily through the ranks of the Royal Engineers – the regiment of which his father-in-law was the commanding officer. He was appointed Knight Commander of the Order of the Bath (KCB) and, at the age of 64, he became Colonel Commandant of the Royal Engineers.

General Montagu had eight children, one of whom survived until 1960. Unsurprisingly perhaps, his eldest son also became a career soldier, rising to the rank of Colonel. Horace Montagu was 93 when he died in the middle of the First World War. It must have seemed to him a very different sort of campaign from the Crimea. His wife survived him, dying herself in 1925.

NOVEMBER 15TH

2010: Colchester Council installed recording equipment in the home of 71-year-old Brian Hockley on this day. The aim was to assess just how much of a nuisance his next-door neighbour's two dogs were. The answer was, a very great nuisance indeed!

Between November 22nd and November 30th, the barking took place a total of sixty-three times between 9 p.m. and 7 a.m. Mr Hockley, who had only contacted the council as a last resort, said:

> It was absolute hell. It was all day long while [my neighbour] was at work, but it got particularly bad at night. I couldn't sleep and it was a big problem. I became quite ill and so I had to get hold of the environmental people.

John Barrett, owner of the Jack Russell and German Shepherd, was eventually summoned to appear at Colchester Magistrates' Court. He sent in a written statement in which he told the court that he did not hear the dogs himself at night and had spent almost £1,000 on obedience classes. He agreed to dispose of the offending animals and was fined £150 with £150 costs. Mr Hockley did not seem to bear any animosity toward his neighbour after the case, saying that Barrett was a nice lad.

NOVEMBER 16TH

1982: Arthur Askey died on this day. A hugely popular entertainer on the radio, particularly during the Second World War, he got his first break in Colchester; the site of his earliest public performance.

Arthur Askey was born in Liverpool in 1900, the only son of the secretary of Sugar Products of Liverpool Ltd. He served in the First World War and performed in various army entertainments. Showbusiness was his ultimate ambition and, after the war ended, he worked for a while as a clerk for Liverpool Council, before joining a touring company who put on shows in music halls.

The Electric Theatre had been opened in Headgate in 1910 by a company called Grand Electric Empires Ltd. It was basically a cinema, but also staged concert parties and had musical turns during the intervals between films. Piano recitals were also given. It was here, on March 31st 1924, that Arthur Askey made his professional debut as a bit player in one of the concert parties. He was to spend another fourteen years touring various minor provincial theatres and music halls in this way, before his big break came in 1938 on the BBC radio programme *Band Waggon*.

NOVEMBER 17TH

2003: St Martin's Church won first prize on this day from Colchester Civic Society for the restoration carried out there.

St Martin's is an ancient church, which stands only a stone's throw from Colchester Town Hall. It dates partly from the twelfth century, with some parts added in the fourteenth century. During the Siege of Colchester in the English Civil War, Royalist snipers took pot shots at the Roundheads from the tower of St Martin's. Parliamentary cannon fired at the church, demolishing the tower, which has never been rebuilt.

By the middle of the eighteenth century, the church was in a ruinous condition and no services were being held there. Some attempt at restoration was made during the final years of Victoria's reign, but by the 1950s, St Martin's was declared redundant. From 1957 it was the base of a local theatre group, but after thirty years, the condition of the building was so bad that they were forced to abandon it in 1987.

In the 1990s, English Heritage and the Churches Conservation Trust stepped in and today St Martin's is open to the public, with its medieval wall paintings on display.

NOVEMBER 18TH

1840: Two young men arrived at The Seahorse pub in Colchester High Street on this day. The landlord, Benjamin Turpin, was suspicious of them as soon as they turned up. They were driving a light gig, whose horse seemed to be on its last legs, as though it had been driven mercilessly for some distance. They were dressed very smartly and so Mr Turpin rented them a room for the night. However, as they were bringing in their luggage, he noticed that one of the men had a pistol tucked into the waistband of his trousers. As soon as they were settled for the night, Benjamin Turpin reported the matter to the police.

Mr Turpin was right to be suspicious of his guests. Early the next morning, a Mr Whitehead, landlord of the White Hart in West Bergholt, turned up in the company of two police officers looking for the young men. They had spent the night at his own inn, paid him with a counterfeit shilling, and then stolen a cloak and whip before bolting. A search of their luggage revealed fifteen more counterfeit shillings and they were arrested and sent for trial at the Chelmsford Assizes. Other offences came to light and they were sentenced to be transported to Australia; one for fourteen years and the other for twenty-one years.

NOVEMBER 19TH

1944: The final salute of Colchester's Home Guard took place on this day before Lord Lieutenant Sir Francis Whitmore. The Colchester section of the Home Guard was known officially as the 8th Essex Battalion Home Guard and boasted over 2,000 men at its height. As with most Home Guard units, there was a perennial problem with obtaining sufficient and appropriate weapons. The situation in Colchester was never as bad in that respect as in some parts of Essex. One group, run by a naval rating, could only acquire twenty-four cutlasses and were accordingly dubbed the 'Cutlass platoon'. As a matter of fact, Colchester's Home Guard seem to have done rather well for weaponry, particularly of the heavier type. They had at various times, for instance, belt-fed Vickers .303 machine guns, flamethrowers, anti-tank guns and even six pounder Hotchkiss guns.

The Stand Down for the Home Guard came on November 1st 1944, when the threat of invasion had been over for three or four years. At the final parade, held at Chelmsford, the Lord Lieutenant of the county told the men on parade, 'You took a prominent part in the defence of our country at the most critical period of the war. In the name of our County of Essex, I thank you.'

NOVEMBER 20TH

2011: On this day, two shipwrecks took place off the coast of Essex. Curiously enough, the same ship was wrecked on both occasions!

The word 'shipwreck' has a romantic air about it, putting one in mind of *Robinson Crusoe* and *Treasure Island*. The shipwreck which took place on November 20th was also near an island, but not a tropical one with pirates milling around. In fact, it was within sight of Mersea Island, which lies a few hundred yards off the Essex coast. Fortunately, Mersea Island is not deserted, it is in fact the easternmost inhabited island of the British Isles. That being so, help was swiftly at hand when the ship was wrecked for the second time in one day.

The trawler *Tavener* ran aground for the first time in the estuary of the River Colne. The tides at this point in the river mean that the water level rises and falls pretty dramatically and if one misjudges it, it is easy to become mired in the thick mud at the mouth of the Colne. It was simply a matter of waiting until the tide changed and, when it did, the *Tavener* was soon on her way. She sailed round Mersea Island and then promptly ran aground again at the entrance to the Blackwater River. The lifeboat from West Mersea was launched and having ascertained that the two crew members were safe, suggested that it might be best to wait for the tide to turn again.

NOVEMBER 21ST

1977: A five-day poetry event which took place at the University of Essex started on this day. It was notable more for the performance of punk music than the reading of carefully crafted Petrarchan sonnets. The Damned and The Stranglers had both played at the university over the summer of that year.

No record has survived of the other poetry read at the event, but there exists a detailed account of musician and songwriter Jimmy Campbell's performance at the five-day festival. Campbell was from Liverpool and had played in several groups, including The Kirkbys, 23rd Turnoff, and Rockin' Horse. An earlier group of which he had been a founder member while still at school, The Panthers, supported the Beatles at a concert in 1962.

At the university poetry festival, Jimmy Campbell accompanied his own songs with just an acoustic guitar. It was a very small scale event, with no more than thirty of forty in the audience, and those who were there said that the atmosphere was more like a private party than anything else.

NOVEMBER 22ND

1883: Over 160 geese were shot on Mersea Island on this day.

These days, we tend to hunt down wild birds with the aim of observing them in their natural habitat; perhaps taking a few photographs of them. The Victorians had a rather more robust and active approach. A large wild bird flying around meant an opportunity to display one's marksmanship, while providing a tasty dinner at the same time.

According to the records of the Essex Field Club, a Mr Musset of West Mersea was hunting with some friends near the Blackwater River. The day was foggy, but this did not prevent the party from bagging 160 geese.

The following is an account of another goose-hunting expedition at the mouth of the Blackwater:

> A vast herd of these birds had collected on the ooze to feed. All the local punt-gunners, to the number of a dozen, were attracted by the sight and setting together to the geese, just as they were densely packed on the last bit of feeding ground left by the rising tide, aimed and fired by signal. The result was that the gunners picked up close on 300 fowl.

November 23rd

2001: This is the day that Mary Whitehousedied in a Colchester nursing home. A devout Christian, Mary Whitehouse did not become famous until she was in her mid fifties. In 1964, when she was 54, she founded the 'Clean up TV Campaign', which, the following year, became the National Viewers and Listeners Association.

Although a figure of fun for many, Mary Whitehouse made a number of points which the passage of years have shown to be perfectly valid. She argued, for example, that constant exposure to violence on television has the effect of desensitizing people to real life violence.

Made a CBE in 1980, Mary Whitehouse resigned as chair of the National Viewers and Listeners Association in 1994, when she was 84. Five years later, she and her husband moved together into a nursing home in Colchester, where her husband died the following year. She survived him by a matter of months, dying at the age of 91 in 2001.

November 24th

1905: The Grand Theatre, which had opened earlier that year in Colchester, changed its name on this day to The Grand Palace of Varieties. It is thought that after spending a few initial months as a straightforward theatre, the management realised that they were unlikely to make enough money to break even and so decided to switch to a music hall type venue. A year later, the name was changed again, this time to the Hippodrome.

It is seldom a promising sign when any place of entertainment changes its name three times in eighteen months. The Hippodrome, as it became, had seating for 1,700 patrons and a luxurious interior; it just did not seem to appeal to the citizens of Colchester. It limped on for a dozen years until the end of the First World War and then, in 1920, became a cinema. A few years later, it was acquired by the Gaumont chain and remained one of their cinemas until 1961, when it was converted into a bingo hall.

When Top Rank sold the building in 1985, it stood empty for three years; reopening in 1988 as a nightclub called The Big R. This did not succeed and the Hippodrome changed hands again two years later. It has since been renamed the Hippodrome and is currently a discotheque.

NOVEMBER 25TH

1971: The *Daily Telegraph* reported on this day that University of Essex Gay Lib had started a club and were hoping that soldiers based in Colchester might wish to join. It is hard today to realise what a revolutionary idea a gay club was forty years ago. As far as the *Telegraph* was concerned, it epitomised everything that people had been saying for years about universities like that at Essex!

Homosexual acts between consenting adults in private had been legalised in the late 1960s, but it was still technically possible for two men to be arrested for kissing in public. No public house would tolerate behaviour of this kind; as much from fear of police attention as anything else. As a result, many gay people were forced to live a furtive existence. It was still fairly common for overtly homosexual men to be picked on, bullied and even beaten up in the street. The idea of openly advertising a club where gay people could hang out freely and openly was a radical one indeed, especially in a garrison town whose squaddies were not exactly renowned for their tolerant attitude towards such goings on!

November 26th

1628: Samuel Harsnett was proclaimed Archbishop of York on this day. Harsnett came from a very humble background; his father was a baker. He was born in the St Botolph's parish of Colchester and as a boy, attended what is now the Colchester Royal Grammar School. He was enrolled at Cambridge University at the exceedingly young age of 15, which enabled him to graduate before his 20th birthday. He was only 22 when he was ordained in the Church of England.

In 1587, when he was 26, Samuel Harsnett returned to Colchester and became the head of the grammar school. The next year, he resigned from what he described as 'the painful trade of teaching'. His career in the Church was extraordinary. He became Bishop of Chichester, Bishop of Norwich and then, finally, Archbishop of York. He died three years later, at the then fairly advanced age of 70. He is buried in Chigwell.

NOVEMBER 27TH

2011: On this day, Carla Bottle wrote to Colchester Council thanking them for information with which they had provided her about stray dogs in the town. On October 11th 2011, she had made a Freedom of Information request to the council, asking them how many stray dogs they had taken to the pound in 2010, how many had been reclaimed by their owners, whether or not any had been 'euthanized', and how many had been adopted, sent to animal rescue or had been taken to the pound on more than one occasion. Oh, and she also wanted a breakdown of the different breeds as well.

It is impossible to speculate as to Ms Bottle's reasons for wanting so detailed an account of the fate of stray dogs found in Colchester. Under the Freedom of Information Act, one is not obliged to give reasons; merely to ask for the information.

For those who wish to know, 335 stray dogs were taken to the pound in 2010, of which 160 were subsequently reunited with their owners. Sixty-seven of the remaining dogs were adopted and none went to animal rescue centres. Fifty-three dogs were destroyed. Whoever sent the information slipped in the blunt statement that the breeds of all dogs were recorded; presumably hoping and praying that Ms Bottle would not then ask to know the actual breeds of all 335 animals. In the event, she did not, and merely thanked them politely for the information which they had furnished.

NOVEMBER 28TH

2011: At precisely 10 a.m. on this day a new gallery dedicated to Colchester-made clocks and watches opened at Colchester's Hollytrees Museum. Businessman Bernard Mason donated his collection of timepieces to the people of Colchester in 1979 and the new gallery was accordingly named in his honour.

The timepieces, some of which had previously been displayed in the Tymperley's Museum, dated from the seventeenth to nineteenth centuries. They include long-case clocks (better known as grandfather clocks), lantern clocks and various pocket watches. Bernard Mason began collecting clocks and watches made in Colchester in 1927. His interest in the subject verged on the obsessive and together with his wife, Evelyn, he researched the history of the town's clockmakers in exhaustive detail. The fruits of this forty-year-long labour of love were published in 1969 in his book *Clock and Watchmaking in Colchester*. Mason claimed that 375 Colchester-made clocks still exist; 216 of which he owned. Bernard Mason died in 1981.

NOVEMBER 29TH

2011: On this day, the NHS UK site announced the results of a study, which suggested that 75 per cent of British-grown oysters are contaminated by the norovirus. This is very unnerving for a town like Colchester, which has such an historic association with oysters.

The study was conducted by the Centre for the Environment, Fisheries and Aquaculture Science, working on behalf of the Food Standards Agency. Oysters were randomly sampled from a total of thirty-nine oyster harvesting beds and 76 per cent of the samples were found to contain norovirus. In 52 per cent of the samples, the virus was detected at extremely low levels, but as no safe lower limit for this virus has been established, this may not be significant.

Norovirus causes symptoms similar to food poisoning and so its presence in British oysters was alarming. However, in a throw-away remark which might indicate that there is nothing much to worry about, experts from the Food Standards Agency said that it was difficult to assess the implications of their findings as they were unable to distinguish infectious from non-infectious norovirus material in the shellfish tested.

NOVEMBER 30TH

2007: The Haven in Lexden, Colchester, hosted the last of its open days of the year on this day. Held in a community centre, The Haven runs a project supporting those who have been diagnosed with a personality disorder.

Basically, those with personality disorders behave differently from most other people and, in the jargon of psychiatry, 'appear to deviate from social expectations particularly in relating to others'. Some people with this disorder are severely mentally ill, while others simply feel and act a little differently; they may dislike physical contact, for example, or have little idea how to relate to others.

The Haven Centre is a place where people with this condition can just hang out and be themselves. Those attending the centre have shown a marked improvement in their mental health, with a dramatic drop in hospital admissions once they start attending regularly.

DECEMBER 1ST

1898: This is the day that Colchester's municipal electricity supply was switched on. Up until the 1890s, domestic electricity was only found in wealthy homes. Some operated their own generators to produce power for the home. The only practical use for electricity in the closing years of Victoria's reign was for lighting; there were no vacuum cleaners, washing machines or radios that required sockets in the home!

Colchester Borough Council decided to set up an 'Electric Light Works' in Stanwell Street, with the aim of making electric lighting available for every home in the town. It was a revolutionary scheme and they approached Colchester's biggest company to arrange for the supply of the steam-powered generators necessary to make it a reality. James Paxman's engineering works had recently entered into a contract with James Couthope Peache to produce the very machines for the job. Paxman realised that electricity generation was going to be a big thing in the future and wished to be one of the first to provide it to the town.

By 1905, the Stanwell Street Electric Light Works had seven Peache engines in operation and Colchester had definitely entered the twentieth century.

DECEMBER 2ND

1971: In 1817, the house which Francis Smythies had had specially designed and built, was completed. It was called The Turrets and still stands at 89 Lexden Road; a triumphant Gothic fantasy. So remarkable is the property, that on December 2nd 1971 it was granted Grade II listed status.

Built of plastered brick in the style of a crenulated, medieval castle, the house was designed by Robert Lugar (1773-1855). Lugar was born in Colchester, the son of a carpenter, and towards the end of the eighteenth century established himself as an architect in London. His speciality was Gothic extensions to country houses. Francis Smythies, a lawyer and Colchester's Town Clerk, wanted somewhere really individual and distinctive – Robert Lugar was certainly the man for the job! Passing motorists often slow down or even stop to admire The Turrets. Although it is essentially a suburban villa, this private house is absolutely unique in Colchester and possibly the entire country.

DECEMBER 3RD

2008: This day saw the first ever performance of Graham Lynch's *The Stolen Branch*, which took place at the Colchester Institute. Strictly speaking, this is a little misleading.

Lynch was a composer who, after studying music, went off into the Highlands for eight years to mull over all that he had learned. He composed *The Stolen Branch*, which is based upon the following poem by Pablo Neruda:

> We shall go into the night to steal
> A flowering branch
> We shall climb over the wall
> In the darkness of someone's garden
> Two shadows in the shadow

Rather ingeniously, Lynch has managed to generate an apparently infinite series of world premieres from this music. The performance in Colchester, for instance, was the first of the violin and clarinet version. Four days earlier, at Crystal Palace in London, was the world premiere of the alto flute and guitar version. A few months earlier, in August, was the Spanish premiere of the flute and piano version, and back in May had been the first performance of the violin and percussion version, which took place in King's Lynn. Presumably at some stage we shall be witnessing the Slovenian premiere of *The Stolen Branch*, played for the first time on the mouth organ or Jew's Harp.

DECEMBER 4TH

1189: St Botolph's Priory was granted a charter on this day; part of a job lot to raise money for the crusade upon which Richard the Lionheart was about to embark. He signed the document, in exchange for a substantial cash donation to his treasury, at Dover, just as he was about to take a ship for the Holy Land.

St Botolph's, or St Julian and St Botolph's to give it its full name, was the first Augustinian monastery in England. It was founded in the late eleventh century, although it did not receive an official charter until a century later. At the dissolution of the monasteries during the reign of Henry VIII, the church became the parish church for the area. Unfortunately, it was largely reduced to rubble during Fairfax's Siege of Colchester in 1648. It was so damaged by cannon fire that only an arcade of arches remain today.

Because Essex has no stone for building, St Botolph's was constructed of flints, held together with cement and interspersed with layers of Roman tiles from the nearby ruins. This rough surface was then smoothed over with plaster, all of which has disintegrated over the centuries. The ruins are still strangely impressive; it being unusual to see an ecclesiastical building of this size made of flint and tile. The arches and doorways are all rounded in the Norman style and some decorative 'dogtooth' decoration survives above the doors.

DECEMBER 5TH

1991: Abberton Reservoir and the surrounding land was designated a site of special scientific interest on this day. Operated by Essex & Suffolk Water, the vast reservoir, containing 25,000 million litres, is the largest body of fresh water in Essex. The reservoir was constructed by damming a river valley and does nor rely upon natural rainfall. Instead, water is pumped into it from the Chelmer, Blackwater and Stour rivers. At the time of writing, plans are afoot to increase the capacity of Abberton to over 40,000 million litres.

Abberton is one of Europe's most important wetland sites. It is on the migration routes for many different species of birds and thousands stop over to rest here. It is estimated that up to 40,000 ducks, swans and geese visit the site every year. Among the more unusual birds to be seen in the vicinity of the reservoir are cormorants nesting in trees. They have been observed doing this at Abberton since 1981, and it is one of the few places in Britain where this behaviour has been seen. In recent years short-eared owls have also been spotted near the reservoir.

The area surrounding the reservoir is now an enormous nature reserve. Essex & Suffolk Water, together with Colchester Council, have jointly funded a visitors' centre and there are many walks to be had nearby. Two hides provide an opportunity for the dedicated birdwatcher to wait patiently in hope of seeing some of the rarer visitors to Abberton.

DECEMBER 6TH

1189: Colchester's first charter as a town was granted by Richard I (also known as Richard the Lionheart) on this day. Richard had become king in that year and, like so many English monarchs, soon discovered that the Treasury was practically empty. There were a number of money-making dodges available to hard-up kings in those days. Swingeing taxes were one method, although this could prove counter-productive – one only need look at the Peasants' Revolt a couple of centuries later, precipitated by the introduction of the Poll Tax. In the sixteenth century, Henry VIII struck upon the novel scheme of robbing the Church when he ran out of money, but at the time that Richard acceded to the throne, this option was not likely. This was particularly so since as soon as he became king, he set off on a Church-sponsored crusade to the Middle East

One way to raise funds was to offer to sell charters to those villages and towns who wished for the dignity which such documents would bestow. Becoming a burgher and perhaps Mayor was just the sort of thing that merchants and traders in a place like Colchester would fancy – it would increase their importance no end. Richard actually halted his departure to the Holy Land before taking a ship at Dover, solely to give towns the chance to approach him and offer money in exchange for a charter. Colchester's charter cost the citizens £60; a huge sum of money in those days and very handy for a monarch heading off on a crusade!

DECEMBER 7TH

1907: The *Essex County Standard* carried a photograph on this day of John Everett, Colchester's Town Crier. Everett was born in Coggeshall in 1851 and worked as a boy for his uncle, who was a newsagent. When his uncle moved to George Street in Colchester, John moved with him. In 1874, he married Grace Simms, with whom he had seven children. In order to drum up business, Everett would parade around Colchester with a sandwich board, calling out the bargains to be had at his uncle's newsagent. Perhaps it was this activity which suggested to him applying for the post of Town Crier, which became vacant in 1900.

There had been a Town Crier in Colchester since medieval times and John Everett was the last person to hold the post. In the early twentieth-century world of newspapers, telegraphs and telephones, it was clear that the very idea of a Town Crier was something of an anachronism. In the newspaper article in 1907, for instance, his job entailed walking round the town on December 1st while ringing his bell and then stopping to proclaim,

Cold December hath set in;
Poor men's backs are clothed thin;
Trees are bare, the birds are mute;
A pot and toast would very well suit.

John Everett held the post of Town Crier until his death in July 1917. The job died with him, although it has recently been revived as a purely ceremonial role.

DECEMBER 8TH

1943: On this day, at the height of the Second World War, an American soldier called John C. Leatherbury battered a taxi driver to death in Colchester. Henry Hailstone lived in Colchester and ran a taxi cab. In the early hours of December 8th, he picked up two black American servicemen. He didn't know it at the time, but the men were short of money and had decided to hire a cab and then rob the driver. Hailstone's taxi was found abandoned at Layer Marney the following day. The next day, his badly beaten body was discovered. He had been beaten and then strangled.

This callous crime caused revulsion in the district and it was not long before the two soldiers were tracked down. They were John Leatherbury and George Fowler, both stationed at the US army base in Birch. Predictably, they both tried a 'cut-throat' defence, each blaming the other for Hailstone's death. They were tried before an American military court, which decided that Leatherbury was the more culpable of the two. Fowler was sentenced to life imprisonment, but his companion in crime received a sentence of death. He was hanged at Shepton Mallet Military Prison on May 16th 1944.

DECEMBER 9TH

2011: On this day, planning permission was granted for a development at the recently unearthed site of the Roman circus, which was found during building work where the barracks had once stood. Colchester Archaeological Trust intend to build an interpretive centre, which would be roughly where the starting gates for the old race track would once have been.

The future is not all mapped out for this project though, and a good deal depends upon the success of the Archaeological Trust in obtaining funding for further work. Their first step was to be the purchase of the old Army Education Centre building, which would provide the nucleus for their displays. Having acquired this and then moved in, the Trust would then need to raise further money in order to refit the building according to their needs. Essentially, the greater part of the building would become the headquarters of the Colchester Archaeological Trust, with reconstructions and other displays relating to the circus on the ground floor. Plans for the centre also include a café and gift shop.

DECEMBER 10TH

1603: This is the day that William Gilbert, also known as Gilberd, died of bubonic plague. Gilbert was born in Colchester in 1544. He qualified as a doctor at Cambridge University in 1569 and then moved to London. Although he later became a very well-known doctor – becoming Queen Elizabeth I's personal physician – it is not for this that he is remembered today.

William Gilbert was a man of wide interests and he conducted many investigations into magnetism and electricity. His most famous book was *De Magnete* and he is regarded by some as the father of electrical engineering. He conducted experiments with static electricity and also managed to work out how compasses worked. During much of the sixteenth century it was thought that compasses pointed north because of the influence of the Pole Star, however, Gilbert correctly deduced that not only was it was the magnetic field of the Earth which caused the needles of compasses to move, but he also worked out the implications of this. In doing so, he realised that the Earth's core must be made of iron.

Gilbert's interests did not end with medicine and electro-magnetism. In the 1590s, he produced the first maps of the moon, sketching the craters and mountain ranges without the aid of a telescope. He died in the same year as his patron, Queen Elizabeth I.

DECEMBER 11TH

2001: Perhaps the world's least interesting archaeological investigation came to an end on this day. Lexden Wood Golf Club was building a new golf shop and the Colchester Archaeological Trust wanted to watch the preparation for the building, just on the off-chance that something interesting might be unearthed while the builders were digging the foundations. There were some grounds for optimism. The site is near some of the extensive ditch and dyke system which was thrown up in the first century BC to protect the settlement of Camulodunum from attack by the charioteers of rival tribes. A ditch dug in the area in 1952 had brought to light some fragments of Bronze Age pottery.

The finds in 2001 were meagre. A keyring with a copy of a Roman coin, two pieces of an old jar, and some bits of burnt clay. As those who prepared the subsequent report – grandly entitled 'An Archaeological Watching Brief at Lexden Wood Golf Club' – were forced to concede, 'no features of archaeological significance were revealed'. The pieces of burnt daub (clay used to coat buildings) prompted one archaeologist to make the daring speculation that, 'This daub may be derived from a wattle and daub building'.

DECEMBER 12TH

2011: On this day, somebody posted on the UK UFO website to confirm what another witness had said about triangular UFOs being sighted above Colchester. The original sighting had been made on October 1st 2011, and was supposedly of a triangular craft which was glowing orange and pulsating. Others then posted to report similar sightings around the same time. One witness in York, for instance, claimed to have seen a similar UFO on the same day as the first person, although about nineteen hours later.

Then, on December 12th, another person from Colchester said that he too had seen the orange triangle, sometimes above Colchester, but also over Ipswich. There was a definite feeling among those discussing this that 'stealth' aircraft are in the habit of passing to and fro across the skies of Essex and Suffolk. Given the presence of a number of air bases in the area, this is of course entirely possible. However, the fact that these mysterious UFOs are almost invariably glowing orange, the most likely explanation is that they are groups of Chinese lanterns being carried on the wind and giving the illusion of being lights attached to a larger object.

DECEMBER 13TH

2010: The *Daily Telegraph* reported on this day that Bob Russell, MP for Colchester, has a short way with those expressing less than whole-hearted enthusiasm for royal weddings. One of his constituents wrote to the MP, querying the cost of Prince William's wedding, which was due to take place the following year. Sir Bob, as he now is, was apoplectic with rage at the idea that there could be anybody in his constituency so lacking in patriotism that he would start counting the pennies when planning for a major event of this sort. He wrote back to the hapless individual in no uncertain terms,

> Haven't you got something better to do in your sad life? Bit of a spoilsport, aren't you!? What a miserable person you must be!

It might have been supposed that these sharp words alone would have put Sir Bob's correspondent in his place, but just to make sure that he got his message home, he went on to suggest that if the person did not like the wedding, then perhaps he might want to forego the Bank Holiday which went with it. Perhaps, mused Sir Bob, the person who didn't want, as a taxpayer, to subsidise this splendid day could find some voluntary work to do instead of enjoying a holiday. He ended robustly, by advising the man to, 'get a life and stop whinging'.

DECEMBER 14TH

1702: On this day, Sir Isaac Rebow was returned to Parliament as MP for Colchester; which post he held for the next twelve years.

Isaac Rebow was Colchester born and bred. His unusual surname indicated that he was descended from the Flemish weavers who had settled in the town. This, indeed, was still the business of his family and he went on to make a fortune himself from the manufacture of clothing. After the Glorious Revolution of 1688, he was elected to Parliament as a Whig.

Rebow was something of a favourite of the king, William III, who ruled the country with his wife, Mary. The king, who was himself Dutch, used to travel to and from his native country via Harwich and whenever he did so, he would stay overnight at Isaac Rebow's home in Colchester. It was this close association which led to his being knighted by King William on March 26th 1693.

In 1716, Rebow was appointed Mayor of Colchester. He returned to Parliament again in 1715 and remained an MP until 1722. Sir Isaac Rebow was defeated in the election of 1722 and, despite his best efforts, never returned to Parliament. He had been an MP for most of the preceding thirty-four years. He died on September 6th 1726, at the age of 71.

DECEMBER 15TH

1673: This is the day that Margaret Cavendish, a famous seventeenth-century author and wife of the Marquis of Newcastle, died. She had been born Margaret Lucas, into a wealthy family living near Colchester. Her family were devoted supporters of the king, Charles I, and as a teenager she had seen an anti-Royalist mob ransack and loot her family home. During the English Civil War, she went with her family into exile, living in Paris. It was there that she caught the eye of William Cavendish, an impoverished nobleman, also living in exile. They were married in 1645.

Margaret Cavendish turned to writing because she and her husband had little money. Her early writings were on natural philosophy; what we would today call physics. These included *Philosophical Fancies* (1653) and *Philosophical and Physical Opinions* (1655). After the restoration of the monarchy in 1660, she and her husband returned to England, where Charles II made William Cavendish the Duke of Newcastle. His wife became a Duchess, but the improvement in her affairs did not stop her continuing to write. Although she had begun doing so to make money, she had discovered that she had a talent with words and went on to write poetry, plays and more philosophical reflections. She is the best-known female author of the Restoration.

DECEMBER 16TH

1775: Jane Austen was born on this day. Although we know her today as one of the greatest of all English writers, she very nearly ended up as the Rector of Lexden's wife.

In 1802, John Papillon became the Rector at Chawton in Hampshire. He moved in to the rectory with his unmarried sister, Elizabeth. Six years later, the Austen family moved to Chawton and from the beginning there was talk of what an eligible catch the Reverend Papillon would be for Jane. She was by this time 33 and, in the usual way of things, unlikely to catch a husband now.

There exist a number of letters mentioning John Papillon in connection with Jane Austen and it appears to have been something of a standing joke in the family that she would end up as his wife. For example, she wrote, with tongue in cheek, to her nephew:

> I am happy to tell you that Mr Papillon will soon make his offer, probably next Monday since he returns on Saturday. His intentions can no longer be doubtful in the smallest degree . . .

A few months earlier, John Papillon had inherited a large house at Lexden, not far from Colchester. In the event, nothing came of this possible romance and when John Papillon died in 1838, he was still a bachelor. He is buried at Lexden.

There is a curious postscript in that Jane Austen's brother, Henry, went on to marry a niece of John Papillon's.

DECEMBER 17TH

2009: George Batterbury, onetime navigator on the sailing ship *Cap Pilar*, died on this day. The *Cap Pilar*, crewed by amateurs, undertook an extraordinary round-the-world voyage, which started from Wivenhoe in 1936. There was a crew of nine assorted men and women, including a doctor, a student, a gardener and an 18-year-old boy. There was also a married couple, Adrian and Jane Seligman. What nobody apparently knew was that Jane Seligman was pregnant and in fact gave birth to a daughter, Jessica, in New Zealand; halfway through the voyage. The child spent the first year of her life aboard the *Cap Pilar*.

The Seligmans had bought the old square-rigger cheap in Scandinavia and then brought her back to Essex to get her shipshape and ready for their monumental journey. None of the crew were professional sailors and even their navigator, George Batterbury, had a 'day job' wholly unconnected with the sea; he was a Classics master at an Essex school. Sadly, international events overshadowed the whole enterprise and the *Cap Pilar* returned to England in 1938. It spent the next few years mouldering away in the Wivenhoe mud.

DECEMBER 18TH

1556: Thomas Tye, a leading citizen of Colchester, wrote to Bishop Bonner in London on this day. This was during the Marian persecutions, when Protestants were in danger of being arrested for heresy by those loyal to Catholicism and also by those seeking favour with Queen Mary. Tye said in his letter:

> This letter will inform your Lordship of the state of religion in our part of the country. William Munt and Alice, his wife, with Rose Allen, her Daughter, not only absent themselves from the church and the service of God, but do daily tempt many others away from the same.

Tye was most enthusiastic in hunting out those whom he suspected of being less than wholehearted in their Catholicism. Whether he was motivated by religious fervour or just wished to curry favour with those in power, it is impossible to say at this stage.

As a result of Tye's letters to Bishop Bonner and other key people, warrants were issued for the arrest of William and Alice Munt, as well as Rose Allen. They were taken to Colchester Castle and held for trial. Seven other Protestants were arrested at the same time and also tried for heresy. The verdicts were never in doubt and all the prisoners were sentenced to be burned alive. They were burned in two batches; six in the morning and four in the afternoon. The Munts and Rose Allen were burned in the castle yard along with another man called John Johnson.

DECEMBER 19TH

1851: Joseph Mallord William Turner died on this day. He was perhaps the most famous British painter of all time. Born in London, Turner executed much of his finest work in Essex and Suffolk. His most famous works, such as Flatford Mill and the Haywain, were painted in the Dedham Valley; the very border between the two counties. One of his lesser known masterpieces though was undertaken at Wivenhoe, a stone's throw from Colchester, and it is worthy of note for a number of reasons.

The oil painting, 'Wivenhoe Park, Essex', is now in the National Gallery of Art in Washington DC. It is a pastoral scene featuring all the aspects of the English countryside which people wanted from Turner. There is a lake with swans, a couple of people fooling around in the water with a cart, cows, a thatched barn, a cloudy sky and, in the distance, a grand house. It is archetypal Turner. The fascinating thing about this admittedly marvellous bit of work is that it demonstrates clearly Turner's commercial streak. The commission was undertaken over two months in 1816, purely and simply to pay for his approaching wedding.

DECEMBER 20TH

2010: The lowest temperature ever recorded at the Colchester Weather Site in Myland was observed on this day, when the temperature fell to -11.6 degrees Celsius.

Because of its position, near to the East coast and the North Sea, Colchester's climate often has more in common with the continent than it does with the rest of Britain. This means, for example, that very cold nights are not uncommon in winter. In fact, the climate of this part of Essex generally is prone to extremes. It is the driest part of the United Kingdom, with an average annual rainfall of only 17.8 inches. The reason for this is simple. Although, like Britain in general, Colchester has what is called an Oceanic Climate, its geographical position means that it tends to miss out on the weather systems coming in from the Atlantic. Since it is these systems which bring most of the rain to the United Kingdom, it is not perhaps surprising that the clouds have disgorged most of their moisture over Wales and the western half of the country before they reach Essex.

Although prone to frosts and cold nights in the winter, Colchester only averages thirteen years a day of snow.

DECEMBER 21ST

2009: The University of Essex Iranian Society, based at the campus at Wivenhoe, recorded on their Facebook page that this date is of social significance to their culture.

Most Iranians are Shia Muslims, whose beliefs differ in some ways from the mainstream Sunni Muslim beliefs. In their country, though, are relics of older religions such as Zoroastrianism. December 21st is the winter solstice, the shortest day of the year. Many countries have festivals around this time of year, including our own. Christmas was fixed a few days after the winter solstice. According to the Iranian Society at the university, December 21st is called the Shab e Cheleh Festival, and it falls on the last day of the Iranian month of Azar. The festival itself is concerned with birth and renewal, just as Christmas is. The days grow longer from this date and so it represents a victory by the sun against darkness. The sort of things seen at Shab e Cheleh are very similar to older traditions of Christmas. Nuts and dried fruit are eaten and candles lit. Essentially, it is a cultural throwback to an earlier time, with no religious meaning to Islam. Nevertheless, many Iranians celebrate Shab e Cheleh, whether they are in Iran or living in Wivenhoe.

DECEMBER 22ND

2010: Harry Mount recorded in the *Daily Telegraph* on this day a particularly gruelling journey which included travelling by rail to Colchester.

Mount, author of a number of popular books such as *A Lust for Windowsills: A Guide to British Buildings from Portcullis to Pebbledash*. The thrust of the article and his chief complaint was that he had just returned from a rail journey to and from Ipswich, which should have taken an hour each way, but in fact took three hours there and three and a half hours back. Needless to say, the delays were caused by snow.

On the way back to London from Ipswich, the train broke down fifty yards outside Colchester Station. After being stranded in the cold for over an hour, they eventually reached Colchester and were shepherded onto another train to continue their journey. With no warning at all, a loudspeaker announced that the train to London would in fact be leaving almost immediately from a completely different platform. The author of the piece felt that his experiences at Colchester summed up all that is wrong with British Rail.

DECEMBER 23RD

1997: Colchester Council agreed on this day to help set up an interpretation centre at Gosbecks Archaeological Park. Most of the walled Roman city of Colchester now lies buried beneath thousands of tons of concrete, brick and tarmac; it is the town centre. Further out though is open land, beneath which lie the remains of the original settlement upon which Colchester was based; the Iron Age town of Camulodunum.

Perhaps it is a mistake to describe Camulodunum as a town. The Roman word for such places was an *oppidum*. These were large areas full of huts, workshops, animal pens and fields; rather like a hill fort, except on flat ground. There were no walls, only a defensive network of banks and ditches.

The part of Camulodunum which was not within the Roman city did not escape development by the invaders entirely. A chariot race track, temple and theatre were all built outside the main area of the Roman city. There are already some interpretation boards and signs in the fields at Gosbeck. The hope is that this will eventually evolve into something more elaborate, an attraction that visitors will flock to in order to get a flavour of pre-Roman Colchester.

DECEMBER 24TH

1997: At 8 p.m. in the evening of this day, the Smith family of Straight Road in Boxten sold a Christmas tree to somebody who really had left it to the last minute.

Since 1961, the Smith family have been planting, harvesting and selling Christmas trees in their fields. They are cultivated from seed and when they are about 4 years old and a foot high are planted outdoors in the field. They are then left for another ten years until between 5 and 6 feet high; the most popular size for the Christmas tree market. When the business first started, the trees were sold at nine pence a foot. These days, people come from all over East Anglia and beyond to the Smith's farm on the edge of Colchester.

DECEMBER 25TH

2008: The activities of the Colchester Prayer Net not unexpectedly reached a crescendo on this day.

Prayers in the December 2008 edition of the Colchester Prayer Net's newsletter were particularly solicited for the homeless and those who are grieving at Christmas. Joan Davies, while thanking people for their prayers, revealed that while she had been praying on this subject, she had been put in mind of all those who were lonely and forgotten at this time of year. As a direct result of her prayers, she was moved to help arrange a Christmas feast for those who are hungry or alone at this time of year.

Elsewhere in the newsletter, we learn that prayers for international students living in the Colchester area had led to a number of Christian folk inviting such students into their homes for a meal at Christmas.

December 26th

2010: Ian Samuel died in Colchester on this day, where he had been born ninety-five years earlier. His was a rich and varied life. He studied modern languages at Oxford, learning French, German, Spanish and Turkish. Once he had decided that he wanted to pursue a career in the diplomatic service, he added Arabic to the four languages in which he was already fluent. He was posted to Tunis, Beirut and Trieste before war broke out in 1939.

In 1940, Samuel enlisted in the RAF and trained as a pilot. He was involved in a number of hair-raising incidents, which culminated in his being shot down over the Atlantic. After the war ended, he resumed his career with the Foreign Service. After being attached to various embassies in the Middle East, he became Foreign Secretary Selwyn Lloyd's Private Secretary. He was later appointed to the same position for Sir Alex Douglas-Home.

Ian Samuel retired in 1965 and followed various interests, including sailing and also writing the biography of an eighteenth-century soldier. He died, in Colchester, the town where he had been born, leaving behind a widow and four grown-up children.

DECEMBER 27TH

1758: John Wesley, the founder of Methodism, visited Colchester on this day. Wesley rode around Britain preaching during the eighteenth century and he passed through Essex on several occasions.

Wesley was heading through Essex in October 1758. He wrote:

> I rode on through an extremely pleasant and fruitful country to Colchester. I have seen very few such towns in England. It lies on the ridge of a hill, with other hills on each side which run parallel with it at a small distance. The two main streets, one running east and west, the other north and south, are quite straight and full as broad as Cheapside.

Wesley arrived in Colchester on October 27th and stayed for three days, holding a number of services. He then rode on to Norwich. After travelling through Norfolk and Suffolk for two months, Wesley found himself in Bury St Edmunds at the end of December. It is worth bearing in mind when reading about his hectic schedule, that John Wesley was 55 at this time; he had more energy than many men half his age.

On December 27th, Wesley returned to Colchester and took the time to visit the castle, which he described as, 'Perhaps the most ancient building in the country'. It was thought at this time that the castle was Roman, rather than Norman. The following year, Wesley was in Colchester in March and September, and then again in December. Little wonder that today the town has a strong tradition of Methodism.

DECEMBER 28TH

1949: On this day, *The Essex Naturalist* ran reports on the bird life to be found on Mersea Island in the winter. Particular mention was made of the Grey Plovers, which are annual winter visitors at East Mersea and Lee Wick. The author of the article wished to make perfectly sure that nobody thought that he might have been muddling up Grey Plovers with Golden Plovers and helpfully explained that their black 'armpits' made the identification sure and that he could even tell the two species apart with his eyes closed; the trisyllabic whistle of the Grey Plover being quite different from the disyllabic call of the Golden Plover.

Grey Plovers were not the only birds to be observed by *The Essex Naturalist* in this part of the county; fifty Black terns (*Chlidonias Niger*) having been spotted at Abberton Reservoir that May. The most exciting episode was the sighting of a White Winged Black Tern, also at Abberton in July. We are told that Mr G. Pyman of the Essex Bird Watching and Preservation Society 'had the unique experience' of seeing this bird and the Greater Yellowshank both standing in the same pool. 'Surely a European record,' enthused the writer.

DECEMBER 29TH

1886: Thomas Abel was beatified by the Roman Catholic Church on this day, meaning that he was officially recognised as a martyr and should now be known as the Blessed Thomas Abel. Thomas Abel was born about 1497 in the village of West Bergholt, north west of Colchester. He studied at Oxford University, after which he became a priest. In 1528, he was appointed chaplain to Henry VIII's first wife, Catherine. When the king fell in love with Anne Boleyn and wanted to divorce his wife, this led to the English Reformation, because the Catholic Church was resolutely opposed to divorce.

Henry VIII was not a man to take no for an answer and it is a matter of historical record that he obtained his divorce eventually. Thomas Abel was so angered by the planned divorce that he rather recklessly published a pamphlet with the uncompromising title, 'That by no manner of law, it may be lawful for the most noble King of England, King Henry the eighth to be divorced from the queens grace, his lawful and very wife'. Nobody, least of all Thomas Abel himself, can have been surprised when he was arrested and sent to the Tower of London. In December 1533, he was taken to Smithfield and there hanged and dismembered at the order of the vengeful monarch.

DECEMBER 30TH

1925: Some very early English inscriptions were found during renovations at an old house at 18 North Hill Colchester on this day. The words were painted on old beams, which had been concealed centuries before by the addition of a new ceiling. The house itself dated back to the fifteenth century and everything about the writing suggested that is had been made when the house was first built. This is what it said:

A ROULYNG STOON GADYR NOMOS,
IN OUER MEKYL RAT YS GRETLOS,
IN MESUR YS NOLOS,
BYSYD B CRIST OWIRE LORDE HYS CROS.

To the modern eye it looks like gibberish, but we must bear in mind that this is Middle English written phonetically. There was a fashion in the late fifteenth century for decorating walls with proverbs and prayers and this is a perfect example. Translated into modern English, the whole thing is revealed as a quatrain:

A rolling stone gathers no moss,
In over much riot is great loss,
In measure is no loss,
Blessed be Christ our Lord, his cross.

DECEMBER 31ST

1816: On this day, William Withey Gull was born on a barge moored near Colchester. It was not an auspicious beginning, as the child was born into a poor, working-class family with few prospects. Following the death of his father, William's mother made heroic efforts to ensure that her son received a decent education. The boy studied hard and eventually managed to enrol at Guy's Hospital medical school.

By the age of 30, William Gull had been appointed Lecturer on Physiology and Comparative Anatomy at Guy's. It was a fantastic example of the Victorian rags to riches story of an industrious young man making his fortune. It was in his fifties that Gull became perhaps the most important doctor in the whole country. He attended the future King Edward VII, then the Prince of Wales during an attack of typhoid. He managed to save the prince's life, for which Queen Victoria conferred a baronetcy upon him in 1872; making him Sir William Gull, 1st Baronet of Brook Street.

In later years, Sir William Gull was appointed Physician-in Ordinary to Queen Victoria, making him in effect the premier physician in the country. Perhaps because of his humble origins and the struggles which he had had to become a doctor, Gull fought for the right of women to be admitted to the medical profession. Among his other achievements are his work on eating disorders. He coined the expression *anorexia nervosa*. Following his death in 1890, William Gull was buried in the village of Thorpe-le-Soken, a stone's throw from the place of his birth.